ALSO BY FREDERICK FRANCK:

DAYS WITH ALBERT SCHWEITZER   1959

MY FRIEND IN AFRICA   1960

AFRICAN SKETCH BOOK   1961

MY EYE IS IN LOVE   1963

OUTSIDER IN THE VATICAN   1965

I LOVE LIFE   1967

EXPLODING CHURCH   1968

SIMENON'S PARIS   1969

THE ZEN OF SEEING   1973

PILGRIMAGE TO NOW/HERE   1973

ENCOUNTER WITH OOMOTO   1975

THE BOOK OF ANGELUS SILESIUS   1976

ZEN AND ZEN CLASSICS   1977

Readers:

AU PAYS DU SOLEIL   1958

AU FIL DE L'EAU   1964

CROQUIS PARISIENS   1969

TUTTE LE STRADE PORTANO A ROMA 1970

everyone

EveryOne

the timeless Myth of "Everyman" reborn

handwritten and with drawings by

FREDERICK FRANCK

DOUBLEDAY & COMPANY, INC.
GARDEN CITY, NEW YORK
1978

I.S.B.N. 0-385-14357-5 Trade
         0-385-13329-4 Paperbound
Library of Congress Catalog Card Number 77-25590

This is the first publication of "EveryOne" in bookform.
It is published simultaneously in hard and paper covers.
Printed in the United States of America.
FIRST EDITION.

CONTENTS

The drawings in this book are not "illustrations". They were drawn in America and Europe while I was working on the play. Its subject matter and its implications never left me and colored my very way of looking at people and places.

*) Although "THE MYTH THAT WAS MY GURU" happens to follow the text of "EVERYONE" it is not a postscript. It is the story of what compelled me to write this contemporary variation on a timeless theme, and of the discoveries it led to.

Once more — as if I were some medieval monk —
 I have to write this book by hand,
 person — to — person
 to you,
 who, as I,
 as EveryOne,
 must answer these questions
 with our very lives
 before we die:
  "Who am I? What is it that makes
  me into a HUMAN being?"

EveryOne
 is written to be read
aloud

 alone, or better:
 with a few friends,
 for...

it is not intended for the cold intellect,
but to be visualized by the
                    inner eye,
to be listened to by the
                    inner ear,
to be experienced in
                    the heart.

It is more than a 15th century play revived: it is
a perennial myth called back to life... for _NOW_

A MYTH ENACTED IS A RITE!

This rite
is a celebration
of the birth of the True Self
that is neither dependent on,
nor independent of
ego...

It is
a Celebration
of
HUMAN
life ...

EveryOne

The members of the cast are:

The Voice of God
Death
Friends
Family
Treasure
Insight
Every One

Each part may be played
either by a man or a woman.

COSTUMING: In productions this was extremely simple. All wore black trousers and tops. For Death these were covered by the burlap cloak. When one of the cast becomes Treasure, she is vested by placing a tinsel boa or stole over her shoulders. Insight, played by the same person who, while invisible, spoke God's Prologue, appears in a severe white cotton alb.

THE STAGE

When staged at Pacem in Terris (see p. 139) the stage area is almost bare. A low bench stands on stage right, from where the cast will enter. Upstage a similar small bench stands in the center, flanked by two more, a few feet apart. A long bench on stage left rear stands at an angle toward the audience. It is the "home base" for the cast. The actress who will speak God's Prologue from the Heavens has taken her position at the rear and above the seating area.

AN OPENING RITUAL

precedes the play in order to set the liturgical mood which will be maintained throughout the play: all movements are formalized and choreographed. Also diction is disciplined and stylized even in the idiomatic passages.   When the audience is seated the musical introduction starts. We play a J.S. Bach Trio sonata for harpsichord, the rhythm of which sustains that of the ritualistic action of the short three-to-five-minute opening ritual.

As the music starts the cast enters. One of the actors carries a large loaf of bread, accompanied by two candle bearers with lighted tapers. Bread and tapers are ceremoniously placed on the central bench, which thereby becomes the spiritual center of the play. Meanwhile, the other actors who carry the garment for Death and the accessories to be worn by Treasure have arranged these on the side benches. All bow deeply before the Bread, then proceed to light the several candles of the stage area.

Meanwhile, EveryOne enters. He does not take part in the action, but sits down on the small bench on stage right and follows the proceedings almost anxiously. When all the candles are lit, the actors stride to where EveryOne is sitting and bow low before him. He hesitates how to respond, gets up awkwardly and is about to sit down again, when he is gently led to center stage where the others form a circle around him. He kneels down and all stretch their hands over him as in blessing (see p. 143). EveryOne arises and—as if trying to understand— looks each one in the circle in the eye. Their faces remain frozen, mask-like. He is now led back to his bench where he will remain motionless until called by Death.

The others have filed to the long bench where they sit down, straight and immobile, hands on knees, faces expressionless. The actor who plays Death then arises together with another who fetches the burlap cloak with hood attached, and vests Death solemnly: the moment the garment covers him, the actor is transformed: immensely old, bent almost double, he limps to upstage center and freezes.

The music stops — God's Voice sounds from the heavens.

Frederick hauck

Zwillingswurde XI 1976

THE VOICE OF GOD FROM THE HEAVENS:

I AM
WHO SEES WHOLE PEOPLES
MILLING ON THEIR TINY PLANET EARTH
IN IGNORANCE, CONCEIT
CONFUSION, DELUSION
ANGER, GUILT
AND FOLLY

I AM
WHO WATCHES
FROM THE CENTER
OF THE HUMAN HEART...

They made Me into an idol,
one of their countless idols,
a child's bogey,
a lollipop for comfort
a tranquilizer
for their conscience

They have desecrated
their Earth,
violated their Great Mother,
exploded the bombs of their folly
in her vast womb,
poisoned the bloodstream
of her oceans
thoughtless of their child's
tomorrow...

LIFE CANNOT GO ON...
LIFE
CAN-
NOT
GO
ON!...

THE EXPERIMENT OF MAN HAS FAILED!

HIS HEART IS FROZEN...

HE MUST GO!

DEATH! WHERE ARE YOU, DEATH!

DEATH   Everywhere, Lord, everywhere

as always,

reaping creatures

always, everywhere...

GOD   Death! Go now for Every One!

DEATH   Every One?

Who is Every One?

Just anybody, Lord?

GOD   Each one is Every One

No one is not Every One!

Anyone of these here
is EveryOne
Go! Say in My Name:
You hour has come!

Death   Yes, Lord,
          I shall call EveryOne...

          EveryOne!

          EVERYONE!!

          EVERY ONE!!!

EVERYONE   Well, well, hello there!

                   (arises casually, as if awakened)
Say, haven't we met before? Don't you remember?
Wasn't it at, uh...what's his name...Of course! That's
where it was! But that was a long time ago! Things
have changed since then! I've come a long way!
Not that I am a millionaire, of course... but I'm pretty
well off ... I own my own home, have nice kids,
a good car... I am what they call "comfortable", yes,
comfortable... I don't have to worry...
Of course: it hasn't always been easy!
You work at it! You use your head!
You look out for yourself, right?
You get in with the right people...
You take good advice, right?
Sure, you need a few lucky breaks...
but in the long run it all pays off...
And so, at last, I am in a position
most of THEM are jealous of, right?

DEATH   EveryOne!

EVERYONE   Let me tell you: I have known

           what it means to be a nobody,

           just Nobody _ just anybody,

           no different from the rest! But then, at last,

           You know and They know:

           That guy is somebody! SOMEBODY!!

DEATH   Yes, yes! Somebody! (approaches EveryOne)

           Famines, wars, torture

           terror...

           You slept quietly

           while bellies burst open

           like chestnuts on the fire,

           dreaming of gleaming new cars!

           Now it is your turn, EveryOne,

           MisterSomebody!

EVERYONE   Good God! What turn?

DEATH   Good God, he says _

           At last you're "back to God"

           are you?

God is their emergency exit
the womb they crawl back into
when really scared!

EVERYONE   Who the hell are you? You...atheist!...
You communist!...You honky...You gook!...
You nigger!...You jew!

What are you doing in this neighborhood, huh?
Who do you think you are?

DEATH   I? I...am Death...

EVERYONE   Death?... What nonsense! No! No!

DEATH   Yes...
I have not overlooked you
"modern man", dear slick fellow...
I have known you too long...
far too long...

EVERYONE   Come off it! What are you picking on me for!

DEATH   I have known you as high priest in Jerusalem

EVERYONE   Never even been near Jerusalem!

DEATH   I have known you as Pilate!

EVERYONE   Me? A pilot...

DEATH   I have known you _
as all the conquerors

Caesars, Napoleons, Hitlers,
insane idols
and their insane followers...

EVERYONE   Me...! a taxpayer, a home owner...!

DEATH   As Pope of Rome...

EVERYONE   Now you are ridiculous! I'm white! I'm a Protestant!

DEATH   As the "good citizen" of New York, London, Warsaw...

EVERYONE   A Polack yet!

DEATH   In every century, in every place
            you were "Somebody,"
            starving out whole peoples
            of nobodies,
            torturing heretics,
            always to the greater glory
            of the current idol.
            Making your babies
            who burned and murdered
            in their turn...

EVERYONE   Not my Kids, huh! My Kids are fine Kids!
          It's their Kids!

DEATH   Plundered, raped, murdered, enslaved...

EVERYONE   One has to eat!
          One has to make a living!

DEATH   But now has come the end of man!
          How you used to boast
          that man would solve
          all the riddles of the universe...
          and then at last, would come
          the good life,
          the golden age of pushing buttons...

EVERYONE   O.K. so we invented technology!
          We wanted to make the world
          "a better place in which to live"...
          How can you get a toaster,
          a missile, to work
          without pushing buttons!

DEATH   And so you push buttons
          in the Golden Age of
          your conceit,
          your age of limitless
          terror and torture!

28

Too much I have seen
since this century of
mechanized murder started...
Like a greenhorn, I, Death
had to learn to take men
no longer one by one,
but by the tens of millions
force fed like chickens
for the mechanical plucker.
I, Death ... am so sick of Death...
Death stinks in his own nostrils...

GET GOING, EVERYONE !!

EVERYONE   Let me be !
You are Death
You are Time !
Give me time,
I have not done with living !

DEATH   They call that living ...

EVERYONE   I have important appointments,
prominent people are waiting for me...

30

DEATH   This trip has first- and last- priority.

EVERYONE   Look here: I'm willing to pay,

          I'll give you a thousand for each day...

          Ten thousand ...

          Twenty for each hour... you want cash?

          I'll get you cash!

DEATH   No use... I set no store by riches,

          I know no V.I.P.'s.

          Presidents, politicians, professors:

          all offer me this world,

          Popes, priests, preachers:

          all offer me the next...

Not one of these buffoons
can bribe me to delay
for the single blinking of
an eye!
I speak to you on highest orders:
final accounting is required...
Obey! This is the day!

34

Lek Koordman rienhove III 70

35

Frederick Franck

EVERYONE   But ... why?

DEATH   Not of illness, not of age,

           you buttonpusher, moonwalker

           must you die:

           the air you poison,

           the nuclear waste

           you dump in oceans

           your plastic junk

           is strangling you!

EVERYONE   Then let it be sudden!

           Why not a stroke, a coronary?

           They say God is merciful ...

DEATH   First comes the final accounting:

           your balance sheet.

EVERYONE   If death is the verdict anyway,

           then why the slow cancer of an audit?

           A balance sheet of what?

           Of all my life?

DEATH   I always love

           to hear them speak about

           "MY life, as if they owned it!

           As if they were anything

           BUT their little lives.

these funny one-day flies!
"MY life, MY wife, MY cat,
MY car, MY children...
They never stop, they never learn...

Write up that balance sheet
of what you did with life
as long as it was yours
and do it now!

EVERYONE It is unfair! You never gave me
any warning!

DEATH Just list your thousand contemptible deeds
on the right...
the five good ones on the left—
they are deductible...
List the hours you wasted
the days squandered, the spoiled years,
the promises you broke,
the wounds you so delighted inflicting...

EVERYONE How could I do that in an hour?
Death! Have a heart!

DEATH Obey me, like the others.

EVERYONE Your Honor! Reverend! It will take me

Venezia. V. 15. 1973

38

a couple of years to make up that accounting.
Bless me, Father!_ Please, Rabbi!
let me make it unimpeachable!
Mr. President! Mr. Chairman!...
Don't take me now!
Not now, not yet, not now!
Not until I'm ready!

DEATH   Don't yelp, don't pray
            Each thing created
            must by nature die,
            This is
            your day.

EVERYONE   Then, at least, tell me:
            Shall I return?
            Is there ... Eternal life ...
            Is there ... reincarnation?

DEATH   Reincarnation? Eternal life...
            Have you not lived
            through endless incarnations
            in this one life?
            Don't you know yet
            That eternal life
            is NOW?

EVERYONE   Now!

Lord, have mercy!

Must I go all alone into this unknown?

Must I leave my friends, my kin,

everything I own?

DEATH   Ask them! Ask THEM!

Just ask them...

The human brain refuses to know...

EVERYONE   Death, Death...

Just spare me till tomorrow

let me think awhile...

DEATH   No delay!

Some time today

I shall point

at your heart...

It stops.

EVERYONE   Help!

HELP!!

HELP!!

My friends... my friends...

Where are my friends?

Partners in business, comrades in arms,

Teammates, fellow parishioners !
True friends we've been
in war, in sport,
in drinking, in praying,
in loving and playing...

(Enter four friends)

All	Hi, EveryOne! What a nice day!
Friend 1	Gee, you look funny!
Friend 2	Hey, poor guy, what's the matter?
Friend 3	He is trembling, he's shaking ...
Friend 4	Why so nervous? Say, can't you stand still?
Friend 1	Are you ill?
Friend 3	He is crying...
Friend 2	He looks as if he's dying!
Friend 4	A cup of coffee! A double scotch!
EVERYONE	You really are my friends, right?
Friend 1	Don't you offend us, EveryOne!
Friend 2	How dare you...
Friend 4	What do you mean ...
Friend 3	Don't you see how upset he is...
DEATH	EveryOne!
EVERYONE	Do you hear that call!
Friend 1	I don't hear anything at all _ do you?
Friend 2	uh, uh, it must be his fever
Friend 3	Never seen him this way
Friend 4	Always joking, come what may...
Friend 1	Tell us, what's the matter?
All	C'mon tell! What the hell, tell!

Friend 2   Have you been hurt?

Friend 1   Some guy did you dirt?

Friend 3   I'll beat him up !

Friend 1	I'd shoot the bastard!
Friend 2	Tell us what's on your mind?
Friend 3, 4	You know we are understanding,
Friend 3	concerned,
Friend 4	kind
EVERYONE	Then listen, friends.
	I have been ordered to go
	on a long and dangerous trip,
	to give an account
	off all my eyes have seen,
	of all my life has been
	Now prove you are real friends,
	come with me!
Friend 1	That sounds scary to me!
Friend 2	What does he mean, "long trip"...
Friend 3	Of course we can't let him down...
	Let's get him safely out of town!
EVERYONE	Don't you see? It is that balance sheet
	that frightens me...
	Help me with that balance sheet!
ALL	Promise is promise (taunting children's chant)
	promise is duty
	friendship is friendship!

GIOVANNI PIERLUIGI

DA PALESTRINA

PRINCIPE

DELLA MUSICA

Friend 1	I'd really love to... but my schedule...
Friend 2	Same here... I'm so busy I'm dizzy...
Friend 3	If a pal needs a hand, you know
	I'm never slow, but...
Friend 2	Sure! Who gave you that order?
EVERYONE	It came
	from across the ultimate border...
	Death brought the order.
Friend 3	Good God! That makes all the difference!
	How could we know?
	I'd sooner kill my own father and mother
	than go with him!
Friend 3	I'd still go with him part of the way
	if I could be back for church next Sunday...
Friend 4	C'mon! Let's go have a drink!
	This morbid trend in you gives me the creeps!
Friend 1	Hey! Cheer up, forget it!
	I bet you'll be all right by tonight,
	safe in your bed
	instead of dead!
Friend 2	I am your loyal friend,
	but why, I ask you, why
	should I lie down with you and die?

EVERYONE   Was it then all a lie?

           I thought the love of friends
           was sacred as the Host,
           a sacrament,
           instead of hollow words
           that mean: Get lost!

ALL   Cut out the sentimentality
           What you lack is a sense of reality!

Friend 1   Nobody is letting you down ...

50   *Frederick Franck*
     Piazza di Spagna 1974

51

Friend 2	It is just normal human nature
Friend 3	Not a guy in this town...
Friend 4	Who has the time, the inclination...
Friend 1	Who is not choked with obligation?
Friends 2,3	Just go alone! Be a man, be brave...
Friend 4	We'll put fresh flowers on your grave!
EVERYONE	Haven't you sworn that for me
	you'd brave the gates of hell?
Friend 1	Gates of Hell! A figure of speech...
Friend 2	Can't you tell we wish you well?
Friend 3	But if you insist on dying
	It's your funeral, my friend!
Friend 2	Still, I'm sad to see him go...
Friend 3	and so alone...
Friend 1	So... in a way aren't we all dying?
Friend 2	Yeah, but now that we most part
	it breaks my heart...
Friend 1	I still say: Don't you worry,
	I'm telling you:
	tomorrow you'll be as good as new!
Friend 3	You'll be alive!
Friend 4	Let's go! The game starts at five!

53

ALL   So long! ... God speed! ... Take it easy!
       Don't you worry! ..
       Take care! You'll be fine! ...
       Be seeing you! ..
       Have a wonderful trip!!
       DRIVE SAFELY!! (Friends exit)

EVERYONE   This is how you take leave
           of your "inseparable friends"...
DEATH   EVERYONE !
EVERYONE   Family ... my relatives...
           How could I forget !
           I still have my relatives, my family !
                                    (enter Family)

ALL   Oh ... Ah ... Mmmm ... Ah ... Oh ...
      What's up?

AUNT All at once, see,
      we felt queasy,
      kind of funny, uneasy ...

SIS   Yeah, a kind of urgency
      as if, you know, right in the family
      there was a bad emergency ...

AUNT Say ... anything happened to you?

SIS   Tell us, honey, tell us all !
      You see we're at your beck and call !

AUNT Tell us ! Family one can still trust
      if no one else,

SIS   no ... one ... else !

UNCLE We relatives,
      we live and die together
      in close togetherness
      through thin and thick
      for better or for worse!
      As does a nation, a great people
      that mans the ramparts
      against the barb'rous foe!

SIS	Thank the Lord! One's relatives one can still count on, even these days...
Aunt	Yes, thank the Lord!
Sis	You are not in money trouble?
UNCLE	Woman trouble?
AUNT	You never had any health problems, right?
UNCLE	Well, anyway, he must be well insured!
EVERYONE	Oh, I am in so much worse a quandary— But I am so grateful, so relieved you people have come...
UNCLE	Relatives stick together, buddy... It is a privilege, a pleasure...
SIS	to prove it in practice.
EVERYONE	Then listen: I have been ordered by the highest authority to go on a long journey, a risky trip... into uncharted territory...
AUNT	Oh, isn't that wonderful! Success after success...
UNCLE	We, the whole family are mighty proud of you.
SIS	Just yesterday I said to our doctor: that EveryOne... what a genius...
AUNT	no wonder he's going far...
SIS	far...

UNCLE   Far!

EVERYONE   Stop it! Shut up! Stop it!
           This is a trip from which
           I'll never come back —
           and before I leave
           I have to square my accounts
           or I'll be doomed forever...

ENDI LE THEE E TROVERA LOJTELLO DOI NAQU

UNCLE	Express yourself clearly – you speak in riddles... To me it sounds, God forbid, you're in trouble with Internal Revenue... accounting, a trip...
AUNT	You are not jumping bail, are you?
SIS	You are not fleeing this great country?
ALL	God forbid, God forbid!
EVERYONE	Oh, I wish I could flee... No, no... I have to show how I lived, have to state all good deeds I didn't do, list the mean tricks I learned at my mother's knee... have to show the complete record!

Come, help me prepare
my accounting before God...

SIS   You believe in God? Really?
Gee, that is funny! Who would
have thought it of you!

AUNT   Or is God "in" again?

SIS   He wasn't last year, uh, uh, not last year...

UNCLE   One goes to church, of course,
like everybody else.

AUNT   Church belongs to Sundays

SIS   as sex to Saturdays...

UNCLE   One prays together, right?...

AUNT, SIS Right!

UNCLE   So one stays together, right?

ALL   Right!

UNCLE   But to take God that seriously,

AUNT   even the preachers don't do that anymore...

SIS   At any rate they didn't last year, not last year
So you ARE a square at heart!

EVERYONE I am not joking!
Will you come with me, or will you not?

AUNT   Well, you are asking a lot, are you not?
There are limits, that's what!

UNCLE	I never refuse help as such
	but too much is too much...
AUNT, SIS	Too much...
UNCLE	Don't get me wrong,
	but you scare a fellow out of his wits,
	I'm not that strong
AUNT	No, he is not!
EVERYONE	Do not betray me
	ties of blood
	Do not forsake me
	Do not undo me further...
UNCLE	Now, now! You are a strong man,
	You have never been afraid of anything...
AUNT	But don't ask people

what they can't possibly do,

and ask it casually, as if

you were inviting us to the movies!

ALL   We love you good

like relatives should,

UNCLE   But on this kind of trip

a man is alone, see, on his own!

EVERYONE   And you? ... And you?

AUNT   No, no! Even if I wanted to, I couldn't go,

I have to go to the doctor, see,

Last night I had a terrible cramp in my toe...

UNCLE   I just got the brightest idea of my life...
         - This is just between you and me — (Whispers)
         I am so keen to help, see...
         I understand a man needs company
         so... why don't you take... my wife?

Sis   Oh ...!

UNCLE   If you and she could just agree:
         nothing I'd rather see,
         She itches
         to go on trips, like all them bitches,
         to dance and prance

68

and do the town!

Take her along! Take her along!

EVERYONE   My faithful, charming family!

This then is your final decision:

to pack me off and send me to oblivion,

and you stay behind!

AUNT   We stay behind as our sacred duty.

And, frankly,

you should never have asked us

in the first place...but we'll forgive you...

You ask me why?

EVERYONE   Yes, why?

SIS   Because that is the beauty

of the family tie!

ALL   That is the beauty   (chant)

of the family tie

UNCLE   So, go in peace!

And this by way of consolation:

I shall, myself, in person,

pronounce your funeral

oration!

SIS   How nice he can be!

UNCLE   Now, will you take my wife?

AUNT	Good heavens! It is late! We have to go!
SIS	Yes, we have tickets...
AUNT	We have tickets for a show...
ALL	Bye-bye now! Farewell, EveryOne, farewell
UNCLE	May God — if He exists — bless you, and forgive me, who dare only flee...
AUNT	Wait, wait! There is time still for a generous Last Will:

ALL Sit down, and make a testament,
a testament, a testament... (sung or chanted)
You can't forget your next of kin,
your next of Kin, your next of Kin!
That is the unforgivable, most mortal,
original...
Sit down and make your testament...
You can't forget your next of kin
FOR THAT IS THE ORIGINAL SINN!

EVERYONE   Oh, the indignity of these speeches!

Like leeches

they suck you empty,

these tribal idols

that strangle you

with their ties of blood.

But why should they love me?

Did I ever love them?

Did I ever love

anything, anyone,

the way I loved my money,

my goods, stocks, bonds,

real estate,

witnesses to my achievement?

Who else, what else

shed brilliant light,

'round every desire,

gave real pleasure

but you, my Treasure!

DEATH   EVERYONE!

EVERYONE   Treasure, sweet! Come quick!!

It's very urgent that we meet!

✳

TREASURE   Sell or buy! Buy or sell!

Cash or margin! Lease or rent!

(a tinsel stole is placed on Treasure as she enters)

EVERYONE   No more of this now!

Are you listening to me?

TREASURE   Of course, of course,

I'm all ears, EveryOne-dahling,

I toil and toil to make you happy

and all for you, my pet,

just so you don't worry...

for I know you so well,

I know you're always worried.

But really, baby, don't you worry:

Your credit rating is A.1,

frederick franck
XI '76

74   Domenica — Argentina · Roma

In any market, Bear or Bull,
any check you write
is covered to the full...
So, don't you worry, stupid!!

EVERYONE   I am in deeper trouble...

TREASURE   My dearest darling, if ever
you find yourself in trouble
just remember:
There is no sorrow in this world
I cannot console,
no adversity I cannot turn

into glorious triumph;
no wound I cannot heal,
no pain, no anxiety
money can't dispel.
There is no stain
money can't cleanse
with honors, with fame
with capital gains to
MIRACLE BRIGHTNESS!

EVERYONE Oh, my darling, Treasure,
then help me:
I have been called from here
elsewhere...
Today I must show my accounts
to the highest echelon...
a last judgment...

TREASURE Last... Judgment?

EVERYONE All my life
I have loved only you,
kissed, cuddled and caressed you
wined and dined you...
Now it's your turn, come
help me with my final audit,

my love, my Treasure,
my sweet, sweet
Mammon!

TREASURE You have just hurt my feelings,
Sir! I hope you realize...
Not that I ever concealed
that Mammon is my real name,
but never once in all these years
did you call me MAMMON!
It was always: honey, treasure, sweet!

AND THAT MAKES ALL THE DIFFERENCE!

EVERYONE Honey! It is just a name,
What does it matter, what's in
a name, baby?

TREASURE My sweet lover!
Or rather: my sweet Customer,

every time,

two bit swindler

or millionaire...

Now it's all over,

loss or gain,

bull or bear,

snow or rain,

NEVER,

NEVER, NEVER

WILL YOU EVER

SEE

THE SUN

AGAIN!

EVERYONE   This is a nightmare, a hallucination!

You, Treasure, my only consolation...

Look! I am done begging you:

I command...

TREASURE   Oh no! Not me!

I'm too pretty and too little

to fragile and too brittle...

I won't follow you one foot,

you walking corpse

No one cares less

82

about your mess

than I !

EVERYONE   Honey! How can you talk to me that way!

84

TREASURE　It was a bit naïve of you,

admit, to swallow all I advertise.

To think that I belonged to you

from top to toe,

don't you agree,

was not too wise...

My job is just

to KILL man's soul,

to make his life a waste,

to shrink his heart to

pea-size,

to leave the foulest

aftertaste...

And yet, mine is a thankless task,

for just before the end,

at the frontier of the night,

they — sometimes — see

the Light... Alas!

86

EVERYONE   The Light...

TREASURE   But, then, the moment one is gone,

I catch myself another one,

the next...

And as for you;

my final consolation:

Once you are a bag of bones

you'll forget my arms,

my charms,

the wonderful cars,

the gorgeous homes,

your brilliant reputation...

yes, even the Dow-Jones!

Well, so long now!

Have a

nice day!

Have a

great

Judgment Day!

＊

EVERYONE   I CURSE

THE CHAIN

OF WOMBS

THAT GAVE ME

BIRTH !

Death take me now.
Now, now is the time!
Take me now !

No light,   (all lights dim)
no light...
Is there NO light ?
Is there no LIGHT ?
Light !
LIGHT !
GIVE ME LIGHT !!

                  *

INSIGHT   I AM   (enter Insight)

I AM HERE

I AM LIGHT!

Insight is Light—

Once awakened

I grow ever stronger.

I shall stay at your side.

I never flee.

I kill all fear

I survive all deaths.

EVERYONE Insight... only Light,

guide me through my night!

INSIGHT To know you are immersed in night

that is the first glimmering of my Light.

EVERYONE Is the Solution

that I confess my sins,

and you will give me

absolution?

But— what are sins?...

INSIGHT Do not speak of sins as catalogued transgressions...

The life that is not HUMAN life,

ignorant of Reality

is sin.

A state of misery is sin,

compounded of meaningless folly,

senseless acts of greed and cruelty,

the trivial aims pursued

that make man's world

and doom his Earth.

THAT STATE OF VIOLENT FUTILITY

IS SIN,

Where Insight leads,

the dense smog of ignorance

and of delusion,

of know-how without wisdom

and compassion,

of greed and hatred,

becomes a mist, a haze

and then

a Radiance.

EVERY ONE   Lead me there, Insight...

INSIGHT   Then—

let all be still inside you, Every One.

LOOK INTO THIS MIRROR! WATCH!

Be still, and listen

to what will speak

from the center of the heart

that never dies

in any man,

where dwells his Way, his Truth, his Life,

buried deep under mountains

of folly, greed, desire.

Watch ... listen carefully

To confess is : to speak out

all that the Mirror shows you.

EVERYONE Let me confess!

Insight! Hold up your mirror!

＊

I confess...

I avow....

＊

I see you, faces of the friends

whom I betrayed

all through my life...

You trusted me, implored my help...

I thought of my own profit first.

You pleaded for encouragement,

BUT I,

WHO TRUSTED NOTHING

AND WAS AFRAID OF ALL,

I made you doubt your own ideals

and thus they came to nought.

WHO COULD FORGIVE THIS?

INSIGHT You must have worshipped,

adored SOMETHING...?

EVERYONE Oh, yes...

I confess

that I adored
a false and imbecilic idol,
chief of all other idols.
I called it SELF...ME!
I offered human sacrifice to it,
yes, my own children...
THE IDOL HAD BUT ONE AIM:
to impress the whole world,
to be greater, better,
more important than all others,
Not like you! Quite different.
NUMBER ONE!
Number One
had to see the whole world
down on its knees before him
in his unique greatness
I NOW FORESWEAR
THIS NUMBER ONE
FOREVER...

INSIGHT You were a child once...
EVERYONE When I was young...
When I was young
I mocked and I despised

94

95

all who were old,

as if they were a different breed,

ugly in body, feeble of mind _

in contrast to handsome,

eternally young

Me.

Then, as this body grew older,

spent itself in gluttony and greed,

had become "dignified"_ grotesque,

I scorned the generous aspirations

of the young

and preached to them

that LAW and ORDER

I never lived myself

INSIGHT   You NEVER LIVED YOURSELF!

EVERYONE   Their hunger for meaning, justice,

their despair with a doomed

and desecrated Earth,

their horror at being condemned

to lives of serfdom

to computers and credit cards

I mocked and I denounced,

of course, invoking the highest

96

Christian principles

INSIGHT   Who did you love?

EVERYONE I now confess:

I hated all, and called my hatred

"LOVE,"

Myself I hated...

I hated all

Who prayed in other words

to other gods

and I avow

that the God I prayed to

Sundays

and the gods I served Mondays

were different idols,

equally false.

I confess

I had contempt for all

whose shade of skin

differed from mine,

I hated all less gifted

than I _ or more gifted.

and I admit

that I despised all

97

who belonged to different parties,
other factions,
whether an inch to the right
or to the left of mine...

INSIGHT   REMEMBER YOUR PARENTS, EVERYONE!

EVERYONE   I looked down

on both my parents,

poor mortals,

I used them as the alibi

for all my follies,

stupidities —

as if they too

had not inherited

THEIR ignorance, THEIR prejudices,

THEIR DELUSIONS, FROM THAT

ENDLESS CHAIN OF CREATURES,

FINALLY HUMAN, FROM WHICH

BOTH THEY AND I, IN ENDLESS

CHAINS OF PAIN

EVOLVED

And, then, I too handed on

these delusions

to the next generation...

INSIGHT   YOU ARE ALL ANGUISH, ANGER!

EVERYONE   How proud I was
of my noble anger, my righteous wrath,
of those impassioned denunciations
that bred more wrath,
and led from wrath to blows,
from blows to stabbings, shootings,
and ever crueler violence,
and then _ inexorably _ to senseless killing,
to mass murder,
and to that technology of extinction

102

that gives priority to bombs

and clouds of gas and germs

and to that cloud

named SUICIDE

that spells the end of man.

INSIGHT YOU ARE AWAKENING

AFTER THE LONG NIGHTMARE!

NO ONE WHO HAS SEEN

INTO THIS MIRROR

HAS LIVED IN VAIN...

BUT THERE IS MORE TO SEE:

SEE DEEPER, DEEPER

AND THEN
SPEAK !
SPEAK !!

*

EVERY ONE I SEE...
I SEE ...my face...
face...
At last...
without its masks
IT IS THE HUMAN
FACE !
IT IS JUST THE HUMAN FACE !!
HOW I ALWAYS HATED IT!

*

SEE MY FACE ?
SEE MY FACE ?

IT IS HUMAN !

*

At last...
Oh, miracle of mercy,
these eyes have opened...

I see you,

I perceive you!

I see you World, my hell —

Beloved Earth, my paradise —

I have not lost you yet,

I find you all

unspoilt, unspent...

Am I a sleeper wakened,

the blind man made to see?

I see all splendor and all glory...

(entire cast forms open circle around Every One, once
more hands are stretched forth in support and blessing)

Actor 1	I see the children, see through their new eyes!
Actor 2	I see the lovers intertwined, I see through lovers' eyes!
Actor 3	I see through ancient eyes, I see the old and bent...
EVERYONE	May all see the Reality of Being before their end.

```
              Blessed are the eyes
              that mine once met
              and thus for all eternity
Actor 1       Blessed these hands
              that could caress,
Actor 2       the hands that caressed
Actor 3       me, the lips that kissed
Actor 4       mine, without deceit.
EVERYONE      Thank you
              Wife, partner, comrade,
              lover,
              whose flesh
              was one with this flesh
              and made it whole!
Death         YOU MUST END NOW, EVERYONE
              THE HOUR IS AT HAND.


EVERYONE      Still I must speak to all
              of what these eyes
              now see!
```

107

Life does not perish
with me, Death,
for what I am is Life.
YOU CANNOT TOUCH LIFE,
DEATH...

I bless you, Life of my life,
Being of my being,
Reality of my reality

BE ALL EMBRACED,
YOU FELLOW BEINGS!

Actor 1   No more need to kill you, creatures...

Actor 2   No more need to fish you out of streams...

Actor 3   No more need to devour your living flesh...

Actor 4   No more elbow you away

EVERYONE   No more shall I beat this breast

           and shout: LOOK ALL YOU CREATURES,

           I AM THE MASTER OF CREATION,

           I am the greatest on this Earth!

INSIGHT   What is this "I" now?

EVERYONE   I cannot find it... It is gone...

It is no more...

I am now one with all that is,

all who came before

all who shall be —

I AM DISSOLVED

AM FOOD FOR ALL!

The game of "I" is up,

           no longer do I play it

           against you, fellow beings,

           each one growing

           from its seed toward the sun,

Actor 1   bursting out of eggs

           toward your winging,

Actor 2   hanging head down

           from a doctor's hand ,

Actor 3   giving your first cry...

Actor 4   then sucking,

Actor 1   crawling on all fours...

Actor 2   then walking,

Actor 3   talking,

Actor 4   loving,

Actor 1   shoving,

Actor 2   yearning,

Actor 3   learning,

Actor 4   reaching, reaching...

EVERYONE and seeing all you reached
          fleeing, fleeing...
          Closer than brothers,
          nearer than sisters,
          my own True Self.
INSIGHT   AND WHO AM I, EVERYONE?

EVERYONE YOU ARE INSIGHT:
          THE WISDOM THAT IS COMPASSION,
          THE COMPASSION THAT IS WISDOM!
                    *
          How simple is
          the riddle of man's life
          the riddle that I lived
          to solve...

          HOW SIMPLE NOW
          THAT I LIVE
          ETERNITY,
          MY SHORT ETERNITY.
INSIGHT   Wisdom is Life that knows
          it is living!

114

EVERY ONE   AT LAST THIS MOUTH

HAS HALLOWED

THE NAMELESS NAME,

THESE EYES HAVE SEEN

THE KINGDOM COME IN EARTH,

HAVE SEEN YOUR WILL BE DONE!

STILL AM I EATING

THE BREAD OF LIFE.

I AM FORGIVEN, FOR I HAVE FORGIVEN,

LIBERATED AM I

FROM ALL EVIL

FOR THE KINGDOM

AND THE POWER

AND THE GLORY

ARE MY VERY CORE!

Still,
I feel you, good rain,
upon my skin.
Thank you sweet eyes
for seeing,
ears for the murmuring
of water, for wind and storm,
for the hymns of birds,
the humming of the flies.

I, a stone,
I SEE THE STONES
ALIVE,
I HEAR THE WATER
SEEPING INTO THE ROOTS,
I SEE THE LEAVES STILL BREATHING...
I HEAR
THE MOSSES
GROW...

Oh, Timeless, nightless
Life of Life,

these ears already deaf
still hear your awesome singing.
These quenched eyes
still see the brightness
of your Oneness
as midsummer suns,
these...failing...legs
LEAP
across all hurdles
toward....

Is this
the touch
of Death?
So you are real, Death?

You are not real, Death
All is...alive...
All is
LIFE...

      *   (EveryOne's head falls until it rests
           on his chest, mouth sagged open.
           He sits motionless, arms and legs
           crossed as an embryo's.)

THE VOICE OF GOD FROM THE HEAVENS

This play
is almost over, children,
humans
who must die so soon...

Do not speak OF ME,
Ocean of Reality
Do not explain ME,
first and last Mystery

Speak TO ME
and I shall answer.
I have no name.
I am no God that dies.

I am the One
I am the Many
I am in All
you touch, you see,

I AM
THE STRUCTURE
OF
REALITY.

Stop chattering about Me!
About my Son...
Who is my Son
but he who dares
to see Me,

dares embrace Me,
RELENTLESS
STRUCTURE OF REALITY.

He is my Son
whose living flesh
reveals My image,
SHOWS
WHAT IS DIVINE
IN MAN,
Who dies
but knows no death,

122 Holland December, morning   Frederick Franck '69

Fredrick Franck

124

who brings
MY HEALING SPIRIT,
that makes all One,
that makes One All,
MY HOLY SPIRIT.

Eternally mocked
and spat at is my Son.,
Eternally betrayed,
starved,
tortured
gassed,
murdered
is my Son.

ETERNALLY
I RESURRECT HIM
DEEP
IN THE
HUMAN
CORE !

Death, Death!
Stop mowing!
Stop reaping!
Enough! Enough!

EveryOne!
Wake up!
Be reborn!
ARISE!

For you are ripe now
to live the HUMAN life,
to love and live
and glorify...

Go now, Every One,
My Son,
Son of the living
go to the living!
Share my Bread of Life
with all these who surround you,
SEE: THEY ARE MANKIND!

Each single one
here present
conceals, contains,
embraces
all man is!

WAKE UP!
AND SHARE
AND EAT!
HERE IS
THE BREAD OF LIFE!

129

EVERYONE
WAKE UP!
AND SHARE
AND EAT!
HERE
IS
THE BREAD OF LIFE!

The Myth that Was My Guru

As in your bosom you bear your Heaven and Earth and all you behold, tho it appears without, it is within.

William Blake

A play, a painting, a poem—any work of art that manages to survive half a millennium or more, that outlives wars, revolutions, reformations and immense cultural change, must have something of extraordinarily vital importance to say. It must contain something of such timeless and universally human urgency that it transcends even art itself.

The fifteenth-century "morality play," *The Play of Everyman*, is such a work. Forgotten during intervals of peace and tranquillity, this play about the human predicament, about life, death and transfiguration has been rediscovered time and again in periods of stress and despair. Its theme transcends time and place.

I first saw the *Everyman* in Holland, where I was born. I was still a child then. But the play gripped me like a riddle. I could not let go of it, and it kept haunting me through my life. No wonder: the specter of violent death was a constant presence during my childhood . . .

In medieval Dutch the play was called *Elkerlyc,* which actually means "Like Everyone." It was ascribed to a Carthusian monk, Peter Dorland, who was said to have written it around 1450 in the southern Netherlands. But no one really knows whether the play was indeed the work of Peter Dorland or perhaps the translation of an English original first printed in London in 1526.

I often felt that it had to be older than either and that the play probably dated from about the year A.D. 1000, when people were expecting the Second Coming of Christ and the end of the world, or that other "age of anxiety" when the plague was decimating the populations of Europe, and the Jews, accused of poisoning the wells, were massacred in one of the many medieval previews of Auschwitz and Dachau. Bands of fanatics roved through the countryside, scourging themselves, dancing hysterically, murdering and being murdered. The clerics—psychotherapists of the period—sought to allay the anxieties of the hapless masses; through the "morality plays" they tried to offer some catharsis, to give some meaning to this agony of mass death.

Now we are approaching the year A.D. 2000 in our own age of anxiety.

Few believe in the Second Coming (who knows, it might happen incognito and pass unnoticed), but this time the end of the world is all too realistic a prospect, be it with hydrogen bang or pollution whimper . . .

The play seems as pertinent as it ever was.

EARLY INTIMATIONS

My hometown, Maastricht, lies at the tip of that thin appendix of Holland, squeezed between Germany and Belgium. That tip where the three meet, is—in times of peace—a "land without frontiers." Three cultures have mingled and intermarried here for centuries. By the time you enter grade school you speak Dutch, French, German plus the lilting local dialect. Still, it was at precisely this idyllic spot that in both World Wars Germany invaded Western Europe. The first time, I was five years old. From our attic window I watched the red sky over the burning town of Visé, a few miles away. Hand in hand with grandfather I walked along the canal to where, behind an electrified fence and barbed wire entanglements, field-gray German soldiers stood, bayonets glistening in the sun. The constant booming of the Big Berthas seems, in retrospect, to have been the continuo-accompaniment of my childhood. Endless processions of refugees and bandaged soldiers fled across the neutral frontier, past our living room window . . . A bomb from a little biplane with an open cockpit exploded on our neutral playground. I saw the pilot, all leather cap and goggles, as he dropped it . . .

It was this childhood that made me allergic to war and violence for life. As a medical student home for vacation, I saw the strategic Albert Canal being dug just south of where we lived, its banks studded with gun emplacements and machine gun nests. It was 1930 then. Disarmament conferences failed with clockwork regularity. In Germany Hitler had started ranting. I had no doubt another war was at hand and decided to leave as soon as I had my degree. Years of wandering followed. I lived in Scotland, England, Australia, Africa and spent some time in the Far East. And wherever I lived I saw Everyman's fate, this being born, this growing up and striving, this hurried begetting of children and dying. How could one forget it in this one short life of world wars, civil wars, revolutions, genocides and holocausts, of empires falling, religious monoliths dissolving, torture rediscovered as an accepted tool for the subjugation of Everyman's spirit? Everyman had become EveryOne: every man, woman and child in our merciless century.

It was EveryOne who confronted me in white and yellow and black faces; most poignantly in the African faces that filed past during my years as a doctor on the staff of Albert Schweitzer's legendary hospital. Having paddled down the Ogowé river for days in canoes, the sick were brought from their jungle villages, hoping to reach the *Grand Docteur* in time. Often they were not in time, and I saw death's hand close a sick man's eyes, saw his face accept death. Each face was the face of EveryOne, as I was Every-One, and even old Schweitzer was EveryOne. He knew it. For no other reason did he stay and persevere for half a century, till his death in 1966. It was that noble impulse that had sent him, in 1913, to serve those who needed help most.

I saw *The Play of Everyman* again on a trip to Austria between the two world wars. It had been revived once more during that short pause in the continuum of mayhem which by some fluke or other I—and you—have, provisionally, survived. In 1920 the by-now celebrated Salzburg Festival had opened with a new version of the old play by the Austrian poet Hugo von Hofmannsthal. It has remained the trademark of the Salzburg Festival these fifty years, except during the Nazi period, when it was *verboten*.

The Salzburg *Jedermann* was a lavish medieval pageant, nostalgic, roman-ticized, an exquisitely restored antique. But I found it less poignant than the original. It reminded me of Breughel, but of one of Breughel's peasant feasts instead of his phantasmagorias like "The Triumph of Death."

But then, von Hofmannsthal wrote his version in 1911, in that fool's paradise that would explode and vanish forever three years later, when the First World War broke out.

During the half century that followed, Death, one of the play's main char-acters, would graduate from taking individual lives to scything whole scapegoat populations. No longer dependent on illness, old age and natural disaster for a rich crop, Death, since 1911, was to reap a hundred million victims of man-made calamity. Even God, who speaks the Prologue from heaven, would change. The conventional God-image, hardly varied since the Middle Ages, perhaps since the Neolithic era, was to become so ques-tionable after Auschwitz and Hiroshima, that respectable theologians—somewhat prematurely—pronounced Him dead.

But how radically I myself would change from the day I first saw the "Everyman" play to the day when I realized it had been my first guru and recognized it to be much more than a play: It was a myth! Only a myth could have the power to take hold of a child's mind and shape its percep-tions of life. For at least six centuries it had similarly intimated the secret meanings of life and death for innumerable human beings.

I dreamed of rewriting this mythic play for our own age of anxiety; not as a restored cultural relic, but once again as a self-confrontation.

I had spent my childhood on an agnostic family island surrounded by the ocean of Catholic culture of our "land without frontiers." It was a land literally drenched by this culture from the time, two thousand years ago, that Roman legions had camped at this "ford over the river Maas." On the foundations of the Jupiter temple they had built on the banks of the Maas arose, a millennium later, Maastricht's massive, fortresslike basilica of Our Lady Star of the Sea. In times of disaster, famine and war, the bones of St. Servatius, who had been the town's first bishop fifteen hundred years ago, were solemnly carried in their golden casket through the winding streets. At night the families of the sick made silent pilgrimages to the miraculous statue of the Virgin Mary in the basilica. Every country lane had its road-side shrine with a plaster madonna, its iron crucifix from which faded wild flowers swung in the drizzle . . .

Superstitions? Oh, yes. But not quite as crude, as cruel as the superstitions we call ideologies and that have dehumanized us and killed and maimed millions in our century . . .

I felt famished in the serene, agnostic humanism of my parents' home. I had a darker temperament. I was invaded by the Catholic symbolism all around me. I drank it in. These ready-made symbols became the vessels I filled with my first intuitions of meaning. My earliest questionings about life and death were answered by Gregorian chant, by candlelit processions, by *The Play of Everyman*. They kindled my imagination, the more so since I could experience and absorb them in freedom, unhampered by in-doctrination or priestly control. The life-size tortured Christ on his cross on the wall of St. Servatius Cathedral, flanked by two dim lanterns, seemed to speak of the pain of the maimed and the wounded who bumped on carts and trucks over the cobblestones of our town. The Last Sacrament hurried through the rain to someone who was dying, by a priest in lace surplice preceded by a choirboy with a silver bell, spoke of death as Mystery, as having deeper meaning than just "passing away."

Culturally, by sheer osmosis, I grew up as a Catholic, yet I never became a "convert." The word itself was all too repugnant . . . Moreover, my love affair with the Church was one of those affairs that, passionate as they are, must break up, for very early I saw in my beloved too many unlovable habits, tribal, social and political. They frightened me away.

Long before it was à la mode I went Eastward on my pilgrimage in search of clarification. There I found in the Mahayana School of Buddhism to which I gravitated naturally and in which I have steeped myself these thirty years—not as a scholar but as a man—nothing exotic. On the contrary. I found the meanings, the perennial verities, which the Christian symbolism had intimated to me, clarified. It was as if I had traveled to a strange country, where, to my astonishment, I recognized every tree, every crossroad, as if remembered from long ago. In Mahayana I found the split between I and not-I solved, I found its essence of Wisdom-Compassion sublimely expressed in the ideal of the Bodhisattva: the one who, having reached full Enlightenment, vows to refuse his own attainment of Nirvana until he has liberated, saved, all living beings from their suffering, even mice and blades of grass. Mahayana never destroyed, it deepened, my reverence for the greatest of Christian koans: for the first chapter of the Gospel of St. John, the Sermon on the Mount, Christ's "Before Abraham was I am," as it shed its "Clear Light" on that archetypally Christian "Everyman" I could never forget.

Symbols and concepts that differ or even clash in the brain, seemed to fuse spontaneously in the warmth of the heart . . .

And so it happened that when in the fall of 1962 I read Pope John XXIII's opening speech to the Ecumenical Council he had called, I felt: this Pope is a Bodhisattva! It was in the deafening noise of the threats and counterthreats of the Cuban missile crisis that, for once, a man in a uniquely eminent place spoke fearless words of compassion, tolerance, hope and peace . . . words of wisdom that so rarely come out of the mouths of the world's great . . .

"The Creator of the World," said this Christian Bodhisattva, "has imprinted in man's heart an order which his conscience reveals to him and enjoins him to obey." In his wisdom and compassion he too knew he was EveryOne: "I am only the Pope," he said, "I am Joseph, your brother."

Following an irresistible impulse I flew to Rome. I just had to see—and for me that means to draw—this extraordinary Pope and his Council which, I felt, would be a watershed in the history of the human spirit.

The tiny stray bomb that had fallen on our playground had meanwhile been bred, via Hiroshima, into arsenals of multiple warheads. The funny little plane had spawned space probes and missiles. But John XXIII still professed his faith in that which is timeless and "imprinted in EveryOne's heart . . ."

Had the Church, my first love, at last outgrown her failings, her self-betrayals? Was the only spiritual tradition the West had ever adopted going to be integrated, assimilated, applied? Could Christianity, revitalized in the Spirit of a Pope John, at last provide the missing signposts for our confused and nihilistic world? I did not know this genius of the heart had less than a year to live. For innumerable people he never died.

On the very day of his death June 3, 1963, a medal arrived from Pope John in appreciation of my drawings of the First Session of the Council.

Overwhelmed, I flew to Rome that same night. I arrived just in time to draw Angelo Giuseppe Roncalli, Joseph our Brother, a last time . . .

INTERMEZZO: A TWIN PROJECT

By now you may well wonder what all this has to do with the *EveryOne* . . .

The play had become part of a "twin project," if one can speak of projects here, for projects are planned, but these were tasks, dropped into my lap by life itself. They were destined to change all plans and dreams I had for the future. The "twin project" consisted of a play and a place . . . coupled links in the mysterious beginningless chain of cause and effect that shapes our lives and that we can only glimpse in retrospect. Some links I can trace: the Catholic residue of my childhood, my lasting fascination with the ancient *Play of Everyman*, my immersion in Mahayana Buddhism, my impulse to draw Pope John's Council, the medal that had to arrive on that particular day, and a walk through the snow . . .

In the late fifties my wife, Claske, and I were still living in a Greenwich Village loft, where I wrote and painted on the days I did not see patients in the fashionable practice I still kept going, two days a week, in New York's East Sixties. We often drove to Warwick, some sixty miles upstate, where we hiked on country lanes through a landscape I loved, a landscape extraordinarily like the rolling country around Maastricht. The swift Wawayanda river was the spitting image of the Jeker, the ochre stream that flowed past my great-grandfather's house, three thousand miles and many years away.

On one of our walks we fell in love with a dilapidated, tall farmhouse, sitting in a snow-covered meadow on the banks of the Wawayanda. On the broken fence a scribbled "For Sale" sign hung from a rusty nail. The house itself was so deeply buried under the snow that we could not get close enough to peep into the windows. The local agent mentioned a price. I countered with a shameless offer. A few days later a phone call: the offer was accepted.

As soon as the thaw set in, we drove to Warwick and saw that we had become the owners of a terminal case. The deed showed that it had been built around 1840. At one time it had been known as "McCann's Hotel." There were traces of a taproom. The dreamhouse became our nightmare. How could we ever afford to restore this wreck?

The answer came from Providence itself in the shape of a golden retriever, who had lost his way. After hours of search we found his boss: a squat gray-haired man. He was at work on the tall, exquisitely crafted replicas of Dutch windmills, that were his winter business, as he explained in a curious amalgam of Dutch and English. A windmill in his frontyard had the words "Bert Willemse Gladiolus" painted on it. Bert took our wreck into his hands, hands that were a master's. The wreck became inhabitable.

But there was more to it than that: It was to become the next link in the chain. For across the river stood an overgrown, unofficial garbage dump, sloping down from the road level to the water's edge, some thirty feet below . . .

During our first winter, once the leaves had fallen, I saw that the dump was contained in massive fieldstone walls. From a partly collapsed romanesque archway and from deep window-holes, debris spilled onto the banks of the creek. The squat stone foundation looked more like one of the medieval castle ruins around Maastricht than like anything I had ever seen in America. I found out that it had been a watermill, built at the end of the eighteenth century. I bought it for a song.

Here, in this meadow, on this riverbank with its ruin, we could let our roots into the American earth. It was the end of wandering. We had come home.

Returned to Warwick from Pope John's funeral, looking at my dump, I had a sudden vision: I saw its walls restored and rising from these walls a modern roof that in its form would symbolize the flight of the Dove. It would become a kind of sanctuary, but not one bound to any religion in particular. I would dedicate it to the Spirit that had descended on the man who in my lifetime had been the greatest by far—the most compellingly human.

Bert and I started to restore the foot-thick fieldstone walls. We dug out 1,200 wheelbarrows of debris by hand, in order not to damage the ancient structure. I did innumerable sketches, not in a search for form but to recapture what I had seen in my vision. I had to do every sculpture, every piece of stained glass, every mosaic myself. For this was to be one man's uncompromising statement, his artistic "act of faith." I called it "Pacem in Terris" (Peace on Earth), after Pope John's last pastoral letter, the most human document ever to come out of Rome.

Building and carving Pacem in Terris became almost a doodling—a kind of automatic writing in stone and wood instead of paper and pencil—of a series of signs, of tokens, that summed up what I had glimpsed as the meaning of my life, of life itself. As I was redeeming my garbage dump, I felt a kinship with people who had lived thousands of years ago, with the sculptors and masons of temples and cathedrals, with ikon painters, with the prehistoric cave painters of Aurignac and Altamira. If this was to be a work of art, it would be art outside of the art game. If a work of the spirit, then outside the religious game . . . a meditation with the hands.

The ancient Everyman theme haunted me more than ever during those years of building that were also the years in which the Vietnam tragedy was spreading. I had to try and translate the play in terms of our time. What Pacem in Terris was beginning to express in stone and wood was exactly what the old *Everyman* play spoke of in word and gesture. They had become twin links in the chain . . .

As I was building the platform over the pit where the mill wheels used to turn, I saw it as the place where Everyman would die and—in my version—would be reborn. I knew the spot under the apex of the roof from where God's Voice would speak the prologue . . .

Shuttling between the building site and my desk across the river, I wrote and scrapped and rewrote the first attempts at what I hoped might in the end become a "Liturgy of the Human" that could speak across religious and cultural barriers. More and more I felt that the myth embodied in the *Everyman* was valid for EveryOne, maybe now more than ever. It had been my own first guru, but it had interpreted the meaning of life and death to untold generations.

After three years of labor my mill ruin had become a huge sculpture, a sculpture of earth and wood and stone; a sculpture one could walk into, sit down in, where one could become quiet and think and be oneself, meet oneself in the stillness . . . then climb out, renewed, into the sunlight. The ruin had become an oasis of quiet in the electronic din. No one was admitted during those wonderful years. I did not need any expert's advice and we used our savings to pay for Bert's wages and materials—mostly scrap. If the curious insisted in their questions about what I was building, I smiled and said, "A bowling alley." Sometimes I answered, "a Poor Man's Folly."

THE PLACE AND THE PLAY

The deeper I became involved with the primordial myth of Everyman, the more I wondered: Was I writing a kind of poem or a play? As a play it had so little in common with contemporary theater! I could only visualize it performed in a severely choreographed, liturgical style, somewhat like Japanese Noh, that most ritualistic of theaters. Moreover, the tragi-comic interludes of Friends, Family and Treasure in the ancient *Everyman* were somehow similar to *kyogen,* the comic intermezzos between Noh plays . . .

"Was the *Everyman* a ritual perhaps . . . ?"

"Of course it is a ritual!" it dawned on me suddenly. "What else is a ritual than a myth enacted?!"

And this particular ritual was, it struck me, analogous to those "rites of passage" that in all traditional cultures mark the passage from childhood to adulthood and from life to death . . .

Yes, this mythic play is a "rite of passage": from the infantilism of Every-One's pre-human egotism, narcissism and delusions, to that of his fully human status! It is an initiation rite into that which is Specifically Human, that which the Christ and the Buddha have manifested to its furthest, most perfect, "divine" limit. Seen as such, EveryOne in the beginning of the play is the neophyte to be initiated. The frightening personifications of Death, but especially of Friends, Family and Treasure are not cruel carica-tures of real friendship, of real relationship, but projections of EveryOne's own infantile egotism, mirrored for him by initiates in order to lead him, *in extremis*, to the discovery of the New Adam, the New Man hidden at his core. In the second half of his Confession these same figures tenderly sup-port him, speak some of his lines, as does the chorus in Noh plays, which unlike the Greek chorus, does not "comment" on the action, but speaks with the hero's voice.

I am neither theologian, philosopher nor scholar . . . But perhaps it was all to the good to just be what they call an "artist."

For the language of myth is the language of art, a code language of im-agery that speaks to the heart, of universal, timelessly valid insights into human existence, into our relationship to ourselves, to our fellow beings and to the cosmic all-encompassing Reality that is our Ground.

Poetry and, hence myth, speak only to those who have not become tone deaf to the language of imagery. Children always understand it. But the child interprets the myth as a magic tale about strange events and places. The adult may discern in it the life-giving meanings that clarify the struc-ture of his own inner world. When retelling a myth one can transpose it, like music, into another key. But one cannot translate it into those "simple words" that imply factual information. To "explain" a myth is to kill it. Myths are to be listened to.

I listened. For as I had not "made" Pacem in Terris, but found it on my path, so this perennial myth had come unbidden. It was useless to sit down and "fabricate" some play. I had to listen, until the cosmic myth might dic-tate itself.

As I listened the myth which had whispered dim intimations of Mystery, of something Sacred, began to speak to me without ambiguity of benightedness and enlightenment, of perdition and salvation, of estrangement from our essential humanity and its rediscovery and integration. It spoke of our death as a fruit that has to ripen in us, lest our lives be total loss.

It spoke the God-language of Christian myth, and yet it was as if I felt the great Buddhist sages, Huineng, Huang Po, Rinzai, Dogen, nodding their assent . . .

"The Original mind is to be recognized along with the working of senses and thoughts, only it does not belong to them, nor is it independent of them . . ."
"All beings are the Buddha Nature . . ."
"One enlightened thought and the common man is a Buddha . . ."

This myth of EveryOne could, once transposed into contemporary language, be a road sign on our Way, a lodestar for an inner reorientation long overdue . . .

It could give a glimpse at Reality, our reality. There is nothing to be realized but the Real. As my transposition of the myth was taking form it became clear that here and there I would have to deviate radically from my medieval model, however faithful I intended to be to its basic structure. I would have, for instance, to dismiss "Good Deeds." In the old play she calls on her sister Knowledge, who is no other than what we would now call "Insight," meaning "transcendental insight": the Voice of God speaking from Man's core, his True Self. And Insight is precisely what no one but EveryOne himself must call, when at last he has dashed his head against the blank wall of Reality. Another change may seem more radical than it is. The play could not end with EveryOne's death! Having learned what life has to teach, he must be reborn, resurrected . . . I felt that in the ancient play, too, Everyman's death implies his rebirth. For the Cross he crawls to, when at last reconciled to his fate and to God, is not merely the sign of agony and death. Unless it is at the same time the sign of resurrection, the Koan of the Cross is misinterpreted! For it is also the sign of the rebirth of the Unborn, the Undying, of the "Truly Human in this mass of protoplasm that is the human body," to paraphrase Rinzai.

I was often paralyzed for weeks, overawed by this self-imposed task. But during one of these times of aridity it came to me as a revelation that what the myth *really* proclaims is an Image of Man and that the Image of Man it holds up is that of the total, the Whole Man, the unsplit man; that this image is precisely the lodestar, the orientation point we have lost and have replaced by delusive fragmentary images: "secular man," "social man," "political" and "economic man."

When at long last I stopped writing I saw that what I had written—whether play or ritual, poem or myth—was my Credo. To me this Credo is both Buddhist and Christian. Should you judge it to be neither, call it the Credo of the True Man without Label, the indestructible.

FURTHER LINKS IN THE CHAIN

Once Pacem in Terris was finished, in 1966, I showed it to a few of the curious and was astounded by their reactions. I had built and sculpted it for myself believing it was too personal an expression to have much meaning for others. But on the contrary: people came again and again and returned with friends . . . We decided to open it on weekends for whoever wanted to come.

All during that first summer we found men and women sitting silently, taking in the old mill, enjoying the calm of the riverbank. Catholics, Protestants, Jews and even Shintoists inquired whether they could use the "oasis of inwardness" for a service among friends. Shy couples asked, "Could we get married here?" Pacem in Terris had no axe to grind, no ideology to sell. It was just there: a sign of hope, a place of quiet; a place "outta the ratrace" as a youngster put it—which I find the most apt definition of a "sacred space."

Musicians and actors, inspired by the rough stone walls and the wooden roof, which made for exceptional acoustics, offered concerts and poetry readings. Whenever we felt that what they had to contribute was in harmony with the place, it was accepted.

And so in 1970 the stage was literally set for the first performances of what would become the *EveryOne*. It fitted perfectly in its setting. The audiences were moved by it. It became a "success." And yet, these first performances did not satisfy me at all. They were "theater." They were still far from the "liturgy of the Human" I had intended. I had to wait . . .

That same year, of all places in Australia, during a lecture and exhibition tour, I ran into a friend from New York, the Australian-born monk—and born artist—Richard Mann, who was on a visit home. Together we formed a cast and under Richard's direction the play assumed its definitive character as a trans-religious rite. The reactions of both the press and the spectators, or rather participants in the rite, were so encouraging, that we decided to start preparing at once for performances at Pacem in Terris. Returned to America we formed a cast of enthusiastic and committed local people—we did not think in terms of "professional" or "amateur"—and staged it a number of times in 1972. We were invited elsewhere, to Trinity on Lower Broadway, to Montreal, to the Cathedral of St. John the Divine. It was functioning! More invitations were coming in, but our cast of school-teachers, housewives, students and a plant manager could not go on tour indefinitely, and it had to be disbanded.

One of the institutions whose invitation we had declined made a sugges-tion: Could I give an author's reading to substitute for a full production? The experiment intrigued me, and together with Claske, who had spoken both God's Prologue and Insight, I decided to give it a try . . .

We have now given these recitals in more than a score of colleges and universities all over the country, often in combination with workshops on "seeing/drawing as meditation" based on my book *The Zen of Seeing.*

Our simple readings were much more effective than we could have dared to anticipate after the stage productions of the play. We, an oldish fellow and his wife, were hardly matinée idols, after all! And yet, perhaps because we were not acting a play but enacting our credo, we touched some vital center.

It was uncanny: Protestant students and Catholic nuns were as moved by this Credo as were the un-churched. Christians saw it as a Christian play. Buddhists called it a Buddhist play in disguise. Jews declared it to be essen-tially Jewish. It was as if they all rediscovered in it some essence of their Buddhism, Judaism, Christianity that had escaped them, but that became visible once more with all metaphysical accretions stripped away. Ap-parently it did not cause allergic reactions!

A RENAISSANCE OF THE SPIRIT

After readings of the *EveryOne,* conversations followed with old and young people all over the country, and from these I began to realize that the myth I had recognized as my own first guru, reconciled or perhaps eluded the differences in the concept systems, the belief systems, of the various religions. They made me see that it succeeded in this miraculous conciliation by presenting an Image of Man that was implicit in each of these traditions, but that was valid far beyond their constituencies. It was the an-swer to the questions I shared with all those in our audiences: "What makes men different from the animals they hunt?" "What is it, specifically, that makes men human?" "Who am I?" "Who are you?" "What am I doing here?"

These primal, quintessential religious questions contain their own an-swer: They have the very humanness of the one who raises them! For this questioning is what is Specifically Human . . . it is as specific for the human animal to question his existence, to know he must die, as it is specific for him to realize his built-in, imperative demand for self-transcendence: the overcoming of the pre-human ego-self in order that we may attain the True Self of our full human status.

It is as if we human beings were condemned to live in tension, drawn as by a magnet to this True Self, while resisting it and being driven constantly by our animal past, to its evasion.

A UNIVERSAL IMAGE OF THE HUMAN

The Image of Man, which both myth and play express, is a demonstration of this indestructible potentiality of the True Self, of the Truly Human, as lying dormant, all ready and complete in each child born, as its innermost essence, much as the ear of wheat lies dormant in the grain that must die. The function of all initiations and mysteries is to help the dying of the grain, of the little empirical self, the primitive, animal, prehuman narcissism that is the endpoint of mammalian evolution. It is at the same time the starting point of the truly human journey . . . What we habitually excuse as "just human nature," the myth unmasks as being not yet human at all.

But it ends in the celebration of the truly human Nature arising triumphantly from the deadly crisis of the predatory ego-self. The prehuman animal at last has become human! The "True Man without label in this mass of red protoplasm" is at last awakened, the Buddha Nature is liberated, the "Sleeping Christ is risen."

This is not the "self-actualization" of the ego-self, but on the contrary, the actualization of the True Self, the ultimate Human identity that all who are born human have in common. It is the realization of my place in the cosmic process when It becomes self-aware in the human heart. "I am neither I nor other" . . .

The theistic religions Judaism, Christianity and Islam may speak of the realization of this Presence, this indestructible potentiality at man's core, as Salvation, Redemption; non-theistic Buddhism may call it Enlightenment, Awakening, Liberation . . . their constrasting terminologies do not in the least affect the universal validity of the Image of the Human they share and which is perhaps their foundation. The Everyman myth presents this Image, this crucial frame of reference, with a minimum of theological ballast.

And its Image of Man, as valid now as ever, is one of the rare antidotes available against our shallow and synthetic pseudo myths, the myths of eternal youthfulness, invulnerable power, "national security," of redemption by acquisition, salvation by unlimited growth, of the happiness of pursuit . . . False myths are at the root of our nihilistic disorder, as valid myths have always been the foundation of the moral order of societies . . . How far beyond the limping ecumenism of doctrines and institutions is the living Identity of the Human!

These talks and questionings, *in which strangers were strangers no longer,* were—if needed—living proof of the widespread spiritual renaissance that is taking wing. This renaissance is the opposite of a "revival." It is as if a whole generation were on the move, trying to find a way out of a trap.

I learned that there are numberless contemporaries who, allergic to the archaisms of theological language, uncomfortable with church worship, are profoundly religiously moved by the Sacred . . . provided it takes the form of art. They are extraordinarily sensitive to the Numinous on condition that it is experienced as art: poetry by Rilke, Hopkins, Eliot or Basho; the music of Masses by Verdi and Faure, Bach and Palestrina; by Thai Buddhas and romanesque madonnas and Cycladic fertility symbols; by ritualistic theater and dance.

We are beginning to realize that to get out of our nihilistic trap we must dare to reinvent a "religious" attitude to life—our own, our fellow men's and that of the Earth itself. And so countless people everywhere seem to be launched on a new spiritual search, which—if authentic—is none other than the quest for Reality.

In the individual the spiritual search is released and activated by pain, the pain caused by the collapse of our delusion that "this can't happen to me." It is this inevitable crisis in each human life—the collision of the ego and its delusions with the blank wall of Reality—which leads either to cynicism, to the deadness of resignation and stagnation in the prehuman phase or . . . to "rebirth." Rebirth is a wholehearted saying "yes" to life on the fully Human plane of insight . . .

I see the "new" religious attitude to life now emerging as the realization that, not only individually but as a species, we are on a collision course with the Structure of Reality, with the laws that rule the life process of the Earth and of man on Earth. There is a desperate longing, at the eleventh hour for a new harmony between the cosmic and the human life cycles, for the resacralization of what has been desecrated.

A "radical realism" is unfolding. It contrasts sharply with the "naïve realism," that "know-how without wisdom," that has brought us to the present impasse. It is not anti-scientific as long as science stays within its limits of concern with the quantitative aspects of nature. The superstitions of scientism—science misconceived and misapplied—that pretend to offer a coherent world view, however, are as irreconcilable with the religious attitude to life as babble about a utopian unity to be attained. An awareness has been awakened of the interdependence of all that lives on earth. Unity in utter diversity is the fact we deny at our mortal peril. From the Will to Power we are at long last beginning to be converted to a new Will to Meaning.

146

This "life of the spirit," always born in the solitary human being, is never confined to that solitary one, for to be truly awakened is to be aware that the others are as real as oneself, their suffering as real as one's own. Hence, the awakened spirit is unable to ignore the great social dilemmas of our time—war, hunger, the mutilation of the earth. It sees these dilemmas for what they are: at least as much "spiritual" problems—that is, "Reality" problems—as "practical" ones. We are now all too familiar with the techno-logical solutions of "practical" men: genocide as practiced by the Nazis, ecocide as it is committed by the industrialized countries, and collective su-icide as it is being brilliantly prepared by departments of "Defense." It can all happen to me . . .

It is neither necessary, nor desirable to scramble religious traditions into a syncretistic omelet. But more important than the preservation of traditions and institutions in their pure, "uncontaminated" state—as if they had not absorbed untold accretions in their long history—is the reawakening of the religious attitude to life. Equivalences and convergences are becoming no-ticeable, even inescapable, in this time of global communications in which the world is fast becoming one spiritual continent. We find our spiritual home, where the climate is compatible and the heart is nourished.

If my long meditation on the myth of EveryOne should suggest a morose preoccupation with death, I have found it to be, on the contrary, a glorifica-tion of life and its preciousness, in which the mind and all the senses were engaged. It sharpens my ardent love affair with life, that gives me a keener perception of the powder-blue dawn above the black line of pines, the blood-red glow at dusk of another living day. It makes me taste more fully the goodness of bread and cheese and well water. It makes me see the wild-eyed jumps of my white cat in the grass and makes me identify with faces in the subway so intensely that I can see myself seen through those eyes. They and I are the epiphanies of EveryOne. It makes me hear divine reve-lations in Bach's *Passacaglia,* but also in our red chicken Célestine's dark cackle that announces the arrival of her daily gift, an ochre egg; in the trickle of water; in the soft roar of the still-living wood in the stove.

A Sunday morning in Kyoto. It started with my taking part in a Shinto service in the main shrine of Oomoto, a Shinto sect to which some of my best Japanese friends belong. In their liturgy the most sacred gesture con-sists in either two or four handclaps, according to whether it is an ances-tor's spirit who is invoked or a god who is called down. The worshipper, kneeling, head bowed, gives these gentle claps and then his hands remain joined together in silent prayer. I am always deeply moved by this quiet reverence of wordlessness, and although not a Shintoist, I have participated in these Shinto services quite naturally.

Afterward, walking through Kyoto, I entered a Catholic church. It was the moment of the elevation of the Host. People were kneeling, their eyes closed, hands clasped together under lowered heads. Others entered on tiptoe, sprinkled water in an act of purification almost identical with the one at the animistic Shinto shrine. A man crossed himself slowly, pensively. His sign of the cross was a hieroglyphic sign: an invocation of the Human, of the Christ within.

That afternoon we drove to Uji to see the ancient Buddhist temple of Mampuko-ji. Here there was no God to be worshipped, but Sutras were chanted, interlaced with solemn gong beats. Monks sat on round cushions, eyes half closed, hands folded, thumbs touching. The abbot repeated profound bows at the main altar.

Walking out of the temple grounds of Mampuko-ji, I saw in my mind's eye Moslems prostrating themselves in noonday prayer, Hassidim swaying rhythmically, chanting, Sufi dervishes whirling, the devout at Guadeloupe with raised arms as in Byzantine ikons . . .

And as I saw all this folding and clapping and clasping and joining of hands, this chanting and raising of arms, this closing of eyelids and bending of spines and knees, this whirling and swaying, all this holy gymnastics became one sacred choreography. The awesome choreography of withdrawal from all distraction, from all that changes and flows, a turning toward the still Center, the Unborn, the Undying. It was as if the contact of hands caused a short circuit: preventing the escape of all energies to their habitual outward busy-ness, making these energies into wordless signaling from the heart to its Ground, compelling the Ground to answer. I saw it as a sign language that must be part of our physiological make-up, inborn gestures of reverence, of prayer, that are our most intimate means of contact with the deepest layers of the Self, of the Sacred that is EveryOne's Ground, released when in joy or pain we are overcome by Its fascination and awesomeness. Beyond all doctrines, all theologies, these are the gestures of the Human.

I stood in that Japanese temple garden and felt myself surrounded by the 125 million Japanese who crowd these narrow islands, thirteen times as densely populated as our own country. I was acutely aware of my being an expendable, interchangeable atom in the ever-expanding population on our earth. And I was overawed by the realization that however many of us there may ever be, each one will be EveryOne, each one ever born will be called to attain the Truly Human in its fullness, or will have been called to life in vain, for each one contains the True Man: the unassailable Magna Charta of his human dignity.

I thought of the agnostic humanism of my parents' house. Theirs was the optimistic humanism of decent, good people, based in their native trust in the sweet reasonableness of human beings, unable to imagine what our ghastly century was to bring. They were agnostics but not nihilists. They honored all the life-affirming values. My father was no atheist. He honored the All-Encompassing in awareness of his inability to know Its Nature. "I try to live so that if there should be a Judgment, I would not have to fear it." This he not only said, but lived. His imagination was not perverted enough to visualize the utter horror of the nationally and multinationally structured evil that was to dehumanize mankind and finally threaten to drag it down into collective suicide. He would not have understood if I had said to him: "Beware of the once-born! They are armed and must be considered extremely dangerous!" My mother would have shaken her head . . . But our century has taught us, or else we are unteachable.

Each time I see my play performed—and even more so when we give our reading and I cry out, "Is there no light?"—I am choked by the presence of all those who, in death camps and gulags and the torture factories of "civilized" countries, cry out at that very moment: "Why hast thou forsaken me?" and cry for light in their dank holes. I am overcome by the miseries of those who, starved and parched, must live on, till they die in the destitution that violates the human core. And a desperate doubt flashes through me: Could the ancient myth's validity be lost, where national and multinational structures of delusion and evil have the monstrous power to choke the Human by deprivation, torture and electric shock? Can "the Light that lighteneth EveryOne come into the world" be overcome after all? And I am frightened, seized by terror, drowning . . .

Until after the terrible silence I hear Insight's voice:
"I AM
I AM HERE . . ."

Frederick Franck
Pacem in Terris
June 1977.

Appendix:
The Fifteenth-Century "Everyman"

How universal, transcultural and ancient the myth of Everyman really is I learned in Japan, when the Suwaraji Theatre, a Buddhist company connected with the pacifist It-toen Movement, became interested in *EveryOne*.

As we were discussing its Japanese translation, my attention was drawn to *A Study of Everyman* by Genji Takahasi,* which presents convincing evidence that the roots of our archetypal Christian morality play were not only at least a thousand years older than I had ever suspected, but that its central plot is based on a Buddhist parable: "The Man and his Four Wives" (No. 101 Miscellaneous Agamas), which precedes the birth of Christ . . .

The Buddha said to one of his Bhikkus:

"Every man on earth possesses in himself four karmas . . . There was a man who had four wives. He loved his first wife best, he spoiled her and doted on her. She represents the body. He also prized his second wife. As soon as she was out of his sight, he became worried. She represents worldly riches. He was less attached to his third wife. Still, when she was troubled, he would console her. She symbolizes all social connections: parents, brothers, sisters, spouse and children. The fourth wife he treated less as a wife than as a servant. He hardly noticed her at all. When the Messenger of Death summons him, the first wife shrugs. Number two is almost as indifferent, even mocks his attachment to her as sheer egotism. The third wife offers to go with him as far as the city gate, but not a step further. It is the despised fourth wife who says: 'I shall follow you in life as in death, for you I left my home and parents.' She is the symbol of man's essence, his True Nature which survives death, the Indestructible . . ."

This profound parable became in modified form part of the *Legend of Barlaam and Josaphat*, that remarkable legend of Indian origin which contains a christianized version of the life of Gautama Buddha and which

* Ai-Iku-Shu, Tokyo, 1953.

after percolating through Asia, reached the Middle East in the seventh century. It traveled further and penetrated Europe. Here the ancient Buddhist parable, once more transformed, became the central structure of *The Play of Everyman,* that top-hit of the Middle Ages, which after its two-thousand-year pilgrimage around the world, was to return to the East via Warwick, New York, as a Buddhist-Christian credo.

The play was first published by John Scott, or Skot, of London, about the year 1529. A second edition by Scott and two editions by another Tudor printer or publisher named Pynson appeared during the sixteenth century. W. Carew Hazlitt added "Everyman" to his edition of Dodsley's "Old Plays" in 1874. Fox, Duffield and Company, New York, reprinted the Hazlitt version in 1903; and there have been various editions since then. The text of the play that follows is from the Hazlitt version with woodcuts from the Scott edition.

*HERE BEGINNETH A TREATISE HOW THE HIGH
FATHER OF HEAVEN SENDETH DEATH TO SUM-
MON EVERY CREATURE TO COME AND GIVE AC-
COUNT OF THEIR LIVES IN THIS WORLD, AND IS
IN MANNER OF A MORAL PLAY*

Messenger

I PRAY you all give your audience,
And hear this matter with reverence,
By figure a moral play;
The Summoning of Everyman
called it is,
That of our lives and ending shows,
How transitory we be all day:
This matter is wonders precious,
But in the intent of it is more gracious,
And sweet to bear away.
The story saith: man, in the beginning
Look well, and take good heed to the ending,
Be you never so gay:
Ye think sin in the beginning full sweet,
Which in the end causeth thy soul to weep,
When the body lieth in clay.
Here shall you see how Fellowship and Jollity,
Both Strength, Pleasure, and Beauty
Will fade from thee as flower in May;
For ye shall hear, how our Heaven King
Calleth Everyman to a general reckoning:
Give audience, and hear what he doth say.

God *speaketh*

I perceive here in my Majesty
How that all creatures be to me unkind,
Living without dread in worldly prosperity:
Of ghostly sight the people be so blind,

Drowned in sin, they knew me not for their God;
In worldly riches is all their mind,
They fear not my rightwiseness, the sharp rod;
My law that I showed, when I for them died,
They forget clean, and shedding of my blood red;
I hanged between two, it cannot be denied;
To get them life I suffered to be dead;
I healed their feet, with thorns hurt was my head:
I could do no more than I did truly,
And now I see the people do clean forsake me:
They use the seven deadly sins damnable,
As pride, covetise, wrath, and lechery,
Now in the world be made commendable:
And thus they leave of angels the heavenly company,
Every man liveth so after his own pleasure,
And yet of their life they be nothing sure:
I see the more that I them forbear
The worse they be from year to year;
All that liveth appaireth fast,
Therefore I will in all the haste
Have a reckoning of every man's person;
For, and I leave the people thus alone
In their life and wicked tempests,
Verily they will become much worse than beasts;
For now one would by envy another up eat;
Charity they do all clean forget.
I hoped well that every man
In my glory should make his mansion,
And thereto I had them all elect;
But now I see, like traitors deject,
They thank me not for the pleasure that I to them
        meant,
Nor yet for their being that I them have lent;
I proffered the people great multitude of mercy,
And few there be that asketh it heartly;
They be so cumbered with worldly riches,
That needs on them I must do justice,
On every man living without fear.
Where art thou, Death, thou mighty messenger?

Death

Almighty God, I am here at your will,
Your commandment to fulfil.

God

Go thou to Everyman,
And show him in my name
A pilgrimage he must on him take,
Which he in no wise may escape;
And that he bring with him a sure reckoning
Without delay or any tarrying.

Death

Lord, I will in the world go run over all,
And cruelly out-search both great and small;
Every man will I beset that liveth beastly,
Out of God's laws, and dreadeth not folly:
He that loveth riches I will strike with my dart,
His sight to blind, and fro heaven to depart,
Except that alms be his good friend,
In hell for to dwell, world without end.
Lo, yonder I see Everyman walking:
Full little he thinketh on my coming:
His mind is on fleshly lusts and his treasure;
And great pain it shall cause him to endure
Before the Lord, heaven's King.
Everyman, stand still; whither art thou going
Thus gaily? Hast thou thy Maker forgot?

Everyman

Why askest thou? Wouldest thou wit?

Death

Yea, sir, I will show you; in great haste I am sent
        to thee
Fro God out of his Majesty.

Everyman

What! sent to me?

Death

Yea, certainly:
Though you have forgot him here,
He thinketh on thee in the heavenly sphere;
As, ere we depart, thou shalt know.

Everyman

What desireth God of me?

Death

That shall I show thee;
A reckoning he will needs have
Without any lenger respite.

Everyman

To give a reckoning longer leisure I crave;
This blind matter troubleth my wit.

Death

On thee thou must take a long journey,
Therefore thy book of count with thee thou bring,
For turn again thou cannot be no way:
And look thou be sure of thy reckoning;
For before God thou shalt answer and show
Thy many bad deeds, and good but a few,
How thou hast spent thy life, and in what wise,
Before the chief lord of paradise.
Have ado that we were in that way,
For, wit thou well, thou shalt make none attorney.

Everyman

Full unready I am such reckoning to give:
I know thee not; what messenger art thou?

Death

I am Death, that no man dreadeth;
For every man I 'rrest, and no man spareth,
For it is God's commandment
That all to me should be obedient.

Everyman

O Death, thou comest when I had thee least in mind;
In thy power it lieth me to save;
Yet of my good will I give thee, if thou will be kind,
Yea, a thousand pounds shalt thou have,
And [thou] defer this matter till another day.

Death

Everyman, it may not be by no way;
I set not by gold, silver, nor riches,
Ne by pope, emperor, king, duke, ne princes;
For, and I would receive gifts great,
All the world I might get;
But my custom is clean contrary;
I give thee no respite, come hence, and not tarry.

Everyman

Alas! shall I have no lenger respite?
I may say Death giveth no warning:
To think on thee it maketh my heart sick;
For all unready is my book of reckoning:
But, [for] twelve year and I might have abiding,
My counting-book I would make so clear,
That my reckoning I should not need to fear.
Wherefore, Death, I pray thee for God's mercy,
Spare me, till I be provided of remedy.

Death

Thee availeth not to cry, weep, and pray:
But haste thee lightly, that thou wert gone this
    journey;
And prove thy friends, if thou can;
For, wit thou well, the tide abideth no man,
And in the world each living creature
For Adam's sin must die of nature.

Everyman

Death, if I should this pilgrimage take,
And my reckoning surely make,
Show me, for Saint Charity,
Should I not come again shortly?

Death

No, Everyman, and thou be once there,
Thou mayest never more come here,
Trust me verily.

Everyman

O gracious God, in the high seat celestial,
Have mercy on me in this most need.

Shall I have no company from this vale terrestrial
Of mine acquaince, that way me to lead?

Death

Yea, if any be so hardy.
That would go with thee, and bear thee company:
Hie thee that thou were gone to God's magnificence,
Thy reckoning to give before his presence.
What, weenest thou thy life is given thee,
And thy worldly goods also?

Everyman

I had ween'd so verily.

Death

Nay, nay; it was but lend thee;
For, as soon as thou art gone,
Another awhile shall have it, and then go therefro,
Even as thou hast done.
Everyman, thou art mad, thou hast thy wits five,
And here on earth will not amend thy life;
For suddenly I do come.

Everyman

O wretched caitiff, whither shall I flee?
That I might escape this endless sorrow!
Now, gentle Death, spare me till to-morrow,
That I may amend me
With good advisement.

Death

Nay, thereto I will not consent,
Nor no man will I respite;
But to the heart suddenly I shall smite
Without any advisement.
And now out of my sight I will me hie;
See thou make thee ready shortly,
For thou mayest say, this is the day
That no man living may 'scape away.

Everyman

Alas! I may well weep with sighs deep:

Now have I no manner of company
To help me in my journey, and me to keep;
And also my writing is full unready.
How shall I do now for to excuse me!
I would to God I had never be got;
To my soul a full great profit it had be;
For now I fear pains huge and great.
The time passeth: Lord, help, that all wrought!
For though I mourn, it availeth nought:
The day passeth, and is almost ago;
I wot not well what for to do.
To whom were I best my complaint to make?
What, and I to Fellowship thereof spake,
And showed him of this sudden chance!
For in him is all mine affiance;
We have in the world so many a day
Be good friends in sport and play,
I see him yonder certainly;
I trust that he will bear me company,
Therefore to him will I speak to ease my sorrow,
Well met, good Fellowship, and good morrow.

Fellowship *speaketh*

Everyman, good morrow, by this day:
Sir, why lookest thou so piteously?
If anything be amiss, I pray thee, me say,
That I may help to remedy.

Everyman

Yea, good Fellowship, yea;
I am in great jeopardy.

Fellowship

My true friend, show to me your mind;
I will not forsake thee, to my life's end,
In the way of good company.

Everyman

That was well spoken and lovingly.

Fellowship

Sir, I must needs know your heaviness;
I have pity to see you in any distress:

If any have you wronged, ye shall revenged be,
Though I on the ground be slain for thee;
Though that I know before that I should die.

Everyman

Verily, Fellowship, gramercy.

Fellowship

Tush! by thy thanks I set not a straw;
Show me your grief, and say no more.

Everyman

If I my heart should to you break,
And then you to turn your mind fro me,
And would not me comfort, when ye hear me speak,
Then should I ten times sorrier be.

Fellowship

Sir, I say as I will do in deed.

Everyman

Then be you a good friend at need;
I have found you true here-before.

Fellowship

And so ye shall evermore;
For in faith, and thou go to hell,
I will not forsake thee by the way.

Everyman

Ye speak like a good friend, I believe you well;
I shall deserve it, and I may.

Fellowship

I speak of no deserving, by this day;
For he that will say and nothing do,
Is not worthy with good company to go:
Therefore show me the grief of your mind,
As to your friend most loving and kind.

Everyman

I shall show you how it is:
Commanded I am to go a journey,
A long way, hard and dangerous;
And give a strait account without delay
Before the High Judge Adonai;
Wherefore, I pray you, bear me company,
As ye have promised in this journey.

Fellowship

That is matter indeed; promise is duty;
But, and I should take such a voyage on me,
I know it well, it should be to my pain:
Also it makes[s] me afeard certain.
But let us take counsel here as well as we can,
For your words would fear a strong man.

Everyman

Why, ye said, if I had need,
Ye would me never forsake, quick ne dead,
Though it were to hell truly.

Fellowship

So I said certainly;
But such pleasures be set aside, the sooth to say,
And also if ye took such a journey,
When should we come again?

Everyman

Nay, never again till the day of doom.

Fellowship

In faith, then will not I come there:
Who hath you these tidings brought?

Everyman

Indeed, Death was with me here.

Fellowship

Now, by God that all hath bought,
If Death were the messenger,

For no man that is living to-day
I will not go that loath journey,
Not for the father that begat me.

Everyman

Ye promised otherwise, pardy.

Fellowship

I wot well I said so truly,
And yet if thou wilt eat and drink, and make good
  cheer,
Or haunt to women the lusty company,
I would not forsake you, while the day is clear,
Trust me verily.

Everyman

Yea, thereto ye would be ready;
To go to mirth, solace and play,
Your mind will sooner apply
Than to bear me company in my long journey.

Fellowship

Now, in good faith, I will not that way;
But, and thou will murder, or any man kill,
In that I will help thee with a good will.

Everyman

Oh, that is a simple advice indeed:
Gentle fellows [hip,] help me in my necessity;
We have loved long, and now I need,
And now, gentle Fellowship, remember me.

Fellowship

Whether ye have loved me or no,
By Saint John, I will not with thee go.

Everyman

Yet, I pray thee, take the labour, and do so much
  for me,
To bring me forward, for Saint Charity,
And comfort me, till I come without the town.

Fellowship

Nay, and thou would give me a new gown,
I will not a foot with thee go;
But, and thou had tarried, I would not have left
    thee so:
And as now God speed thee in thy journey!
For from thee I will depart, as fast as I may.

Everyman

Whither away, Fellowship? will you forsake me?

Fellowship

Yea, by my fay; to God I betake thee.

Everyman

Farewell, good Fellowship; for this my heart is sore:
Adieu for ever, I shall see thee no more.

Fellowship

In faith, Everyman, farewell now at the end;
For you I will remember that parting is mourning.

Everyman

Alack! shall we thus depart in deed,
O Lady, help, without any more comfort,
Lo, Fellowship forsaketh me in my most need:
For help in this world whither shall I resort?
Fellowship here before with me would merry make;
And now little sorrow for me doth he take.
It is said, in prosperity men friends may find,
Which in adversity be full unkind.
Now whither for succour shall I flee,
Sith that Fellowship hath forsaken me?
To my kinsmen I will truly,
Praying them to help me in my necessity;
I believe that they will do so;
For kind will creep, where it may not go.
I will go say; for yonder I see them go:
Where be ye now, my friends and kinsmen [lo?]

Kindred

Here be we now at your commandment:

Cousin, I pray thee, show us your intent
In any wise, and do not spare.

Cousin

Yea, Everyman, and to us declare
If ye be disposed to go any whither;
For, wot ye well, we will live and die together.

Kindred

In wealth and woe we will with you hold;
For over his kin a man may be bold.

Everyman

Gramercy, my friends and kinsmen kind,
Now shall I show you the grief of my mind.
I was commanded by a messenger,
That is an high king's chief officer;
He bad me go on pilgrimage to my pain,
But I know well I shall never come again:
Also I must give a reckoning strait;
For I have a great enemy that hath me in wait,
Which intendeth me for to hinder.

Kindred

What account is that which ye must render?
That would I know.

Everyman

Of all my works I must show,
How I have lived, and my days spent;
Also of ill deeds that I have used
In my time, sith life was me lent,
And of all virtues that I have refused:
Therefore, I pray you, go thither with me
To help to make mine account, for Saint Charity.

Cousin

What, to go thither? Is that the matter?
Nay, Everyman, I had liever fast bread and water,
All this five year and more.

Everyman

Alas, that ever I was bore!
For now shall I never be merry,
If that you forsake me.

Kindred

Ah, sir! what, ye be a merry man!
Take good heart to you, and make no moan.
But one thing I warn you, by Saint Anne,
As for me ye shall go alone.

Everyman

My cousin, will you not with me go?

Cousin

No, by our lady, I have the cramp in my toe:
Trust not to me; for, so God me speed,
I will deceive you in your most need.

Kindred

It availeth not us to tice:
Ye shall have my maid with all my heart;
She loveth to go to feasts, there to be nice,
And to dance, and abroad to start:
I will give her leave to help you in that journey,
If that you and she may agree.

Everyman

No, show me the very effect of your mind;
Will you go with me, or abide behind?

Kindred

Abide behind! yea, that will I, and I may;
Therefore farewell till another day.

Everyman

How should I be merry or glad?
For fair promises men to me make;
But, when I have most need, they me forsake;
I am deceived, that maketh me sad.

Cousin

Cousin Everyman, farewell now;
For verily I will not go with you:
Also of mine own life an unready reckoning
I have to account, therefore I make tarrying;
Now God keep thee, for now I go.

Everyman

Ah, Jesu, is all come hereto?
Lo, fair words maketh fools fain;
They promise, and nothing will do certain
My kinsmen promised me faithfully,
For to abide with me steadfastly;
And now fast away do they flee:
Even so Fellowship promised me.
What friend were best me of to provide?
I lose my time here longer to abide;
Yet in my mind a thing there is:
All my life I have loved riches;
If that my Good now help me might,
It would make my heart full light:
I will speak to him in this distress:
Where art thou, my Goods and Riches?

Goods

Who calleth me? Everyman? what, hast thou haste?
I lie here in corners trussed and piled so high,
And in chests I am locked so fast,
Also sacked in bags, thou mayest see with thine eye,
I cannot stir; in packs, lo, where I lie!
What would ye have, lightly me say.

Everyman

Come hither, Good, in all the haste thou may;
For of counsel I must desire thee.

Goods

Sir, and ye in the world have sorrow or adversity,
That can I help you to remedy shortly.

Everyman

It is another disease that grieveth me;

In this world it is not, I tell thee so,
I am sent for another way to go,
To give a strait account general
Before the highest Jupiter of all:
And all my life I have had my pleasure in thee,
Therefore I pray thee now go with me;
For, peraventure, thou mayest before God Almighty
My reckoning help to clean and purify,
For it is said ever among,
That money maketh all right that is wrong.

Goods

Nay, nay, Everyman, I sing another song;
I follow no man in such voyages,
For, and I went with thee,
Thou shouldest fare much the worse for me:
For because on me thou diddest set thy mind,
Thy reckoning I have made blotted and blind,
That thine account thou cannot make truly;
And that hast thou for the love of me.

Everyman

That would grieve me full sore,
When I should come to that fearful answer:
Up, and let us go thither together.

Goods

Nay, not so; I am too brittle, I may not endure:
I will follow no man one foot, be ye sure.

Everyman

Alas! I have thee loved, and had great pleasure
All my life-days on my good and treasure.

Goods

That is to thy damnation without lesing,
For my love is contrary to the love everlasting;
But if thou had me loved moderately during,
As to the poor give part for the love of me,
Then shouldest thou not in this dolour have be,
Nor in this great sorrow and care.

Everyman

Lo, now was I deceived, ere I was ware,
And all, I may wete, mis-spending of time.

Goods

What, wenest thou that I am thine?

Everyman

I had went so.

Goods

Nay, Everyman, I say no:
As for a while I was lent thee;
A season thou hast had me in prosperity;
My condition is man's soul to kill,
If I save one, a thousand I do spill:
Weenest thou that I will follow thee?
Nay, not fro this world, verily.

Everyman

I had weened otherwise.

Goods

Therefore to thy soul Good is a thief,
For when thou art dead, this is my guise,
Another to deceive in the same wise,
As I have do thee, and all to his soul's reprefe.

Everyman

O false Good, cursed may thou be,
Thou traitor to God, thou hast deceived me,
And caught me in thy snare.

Goods

Marry, thou brought thyself in care,
Whereof I am right glad:
I must needs laugh, I cannot be sad.

Everyman

Ah, Good, thou hast had long my hearty love;
I gave thee that which should be the Lord's above:

But wilt thou not go with me indeed?
I pray thee truth to say.

Goods

No, so God me speed;
Therefore farewell, and have a good day.

Everyman

Oh, to whom shall I make my moan,
For to go with me in that heavy journey?
First Fellowship he said he would with me gone;
His words were very pleasant and gay,
But afterward he left me alone.
Then spake I to my kinsmen all in despair,
And also they gave me words fair,
They lacked no fair speaking;
But all forsake me in the ending.
Then went I to my Goods that I loved best,
In hope to have found comfort; but there had I least:
For my Goods sharply did me tell,
That he bringeth many in hell.
Then of myself I was ashamed,
And so I am worthy to be blamed:
Thus may I well myself hate.
Of whom shall I now counsel take?
I think that I shall never speed,
Till that I go to my Good Deed;
But, alas! she is so weak,
That she can nother go nor speak:
Yet will I venter on her now.
My Good Deeds, where be you?

Good Deeds

Here I lie cold in the ground;
Thy sins have me so sore bound,
That I cannot stir.

Everyman

O Good Deeds, I stand in great fear;
I must you pray of counsel,
For help now should come right well.

Good Deeds

Everyman, I have understanding,
That thou art summoned account to make
Before Messias of Jerusalem King;
And you do by me, that journey with you will I take.

Everyman

Therefore I come to you my moan to make:
I pray you, that ye will go with me.

Good Deeds

I would full fain, but I cannot stand verily.

Everyman

Why, is there anything on you fall?

Good Deeds

Yea, sir, I may thank you of all;
If ye had perfectly cheered me,
Your book of account full ready now had be.
Look, the books of your works and deeds eke!
Behold how they lie under the feet,
To your soul's heaviness.

Everyman

Our Lord Jesus help me,
For one letter herein can I not see.

Good Deeds

Here is a blind reckoning in time of distress!

Everyman

Good Deeds, I pray you, help me in this need,
Or else I am for ever damned indeed;
Therefore help me to make my reckoning
Before the Redeemer of all thing,
That king is, and was, and ever shall.

Good Deeds

Everyman, I am sorry of your fall,
And fain would I help you, and I were able.

Everyman

Good Deeds, your counsel, I pray you, give me.

Good Deeds

That shall I do verily:
Though that on my feet I may not go,
I have a sister that shall with you also,
Called Knowledge, which shall with you abide,
To help you to make that dreadful reckoning.

[Enter Knowledge.]

Knowledge

Everyman, I will go with thee, and be thy guide,
In thy most need to go by thy side.

Everyman

In good condition I am now in every thing,
And am wholly content with this good thing,
Thanked be God my Creature.

Good Deeds

And when he hath brought thee there,
Where thou shalt heal thee of thy smart,
Then go thou with thy reckoning and thy good deeds
        together,
For to make thee joyful at the heart
Before the blessed Trinity.

Everyman

My Good Deeds, I thank thee heartfully:
I am well content certainly
With your words sweet.

Knowledge

Now go we together lovingly
To Confession, that cleansing river.

Everyman

For joy I weep: I would we there were;
But I pray you to instruct me by intellection,
Where dwelleth that holy virtue Confession?

Knowledge

In the house of salvation;
We shall find him in that place,
That shall us comfort by God's grace.
Lo, this is Confession: kneel down, and ask mercy;
For he is in good conceit with God Almighty.

Everyman

O glorious fountain that all uncleanness doth clarify,
Wash from me the spots of vices unclean,
That on me no sin may be seen;
I come with Knowledge for my redemption,
Redempt with heart and full contrition,
For I am commanded a pilgrimage to take,
And great accounts before God to make.
Now I pray you, Shrift, mother of salvation,
Help hither my good deeds for my piteous exclamation.

Confession

I know your sorrow well, Everyman:
Because with Knowledge ye come to me,
I will you comfort as well as I can;
And a precious jewel I will give thee,
Called penance, voider of adversity:
Therewith shall your body chastised be
With abstinence and perseverance in God's service;
Here shall you receive that scourge of me,
Which is penance strong that ye must endure,
Remember thy Saviour was scourged for thee
With sharp scourges, and suffered it patiently:
So must thou, ere thou pass thy pilgrimage.
Knowledge, keep him in this voyage,
And by that time Good Deeds will be with thee;
But in anywise be sure of mercy,
For your time draweth fast; and ye will saved be,
Ask God mercy, and he will grant truly:
When with the scourge of penance man doth him bind,
The oil of forgiveness then shall he find.

Everyman

Thanked be God for his gracious work;
For now I will my penance begin:
This hath rejoiced and lighted my heart,
Though the knots be painful and hard within.

Knowledge

Everyman, look your penance that ye fulfil,
What pain that ever it to you be;
And I shall give you counsel at will,
How your account ye shall make clearly.

Everyman

O eternal God, O heavenly figure,
O way of rightwiseness, O goodly vision,
Which descended down in a virgin pure,
Because he would Everyman redeem,
Which Adam forfeited by his disobedience,
O blessed Godhead, elect and high Divine,
Forgive me my grievous offence;
Here I cry thee mercy in this presence:
O ghostly treasure, O ransomer and redeemer!
Of all the world hope and conduyter,
Mirror of joy, foundation of mercy,
Which enlumineth heaven and earth thereby,
Hear my clamorous complaint, though it late be,
Receive my prayers of thy benignity,
Though I be a sinner most abominable,
Yet let my name be written in Moses' table.
O Mary, pray to the Maker of all thing
Me for to help at my ending,
And save me from the power of my enemy;
For Death assaileth me strongly:
And, Lady, that I may by mean of thy prayer
Of your son's glory to be partiner.
By the mean of his passion I it crave;
I beseek you help me my soul to save.
Knowledge, give me the scourge of penance,
My flesh therewith shall give acquittance;
I will now begin, if God give me grace.

Knowledge

Everyman, God give you time and space!
Thus I bequeath you in the hands of our Saviour;
Now may you make your reckoning sure.

Everyman

In the name of all the Holy Trinity,
My body punished sore shall be,
Take this body for the sin of the flesh;

Also thou delightest to go gay and fresh;
And in the way of damnation thou did me bring,
Therefore suffer now strokes and punishing:
Now of penance I will wade the water clear,
To save me from purgatory, that sharp fire.

Good Deeds

I thank God, now I can walk and go,
And am delivered of my sickness and woe;
Therefore with Everyman I will go, and not spare,
His good works I will help him to declare.

Knowledge

Now, Everyman, be merry and glad;
Your Good Deeds cometh now, ye may not be sad:
Now is your Good Deeds whole and sound,
Going upright upon the ground.

Everyman

My heart is light, and shall be evermore;
Now will I smite faster than I did before.

Good Deeds

Everyman pilgrim, my special friend,
Blessed be thou without end;
For thee is prepared the eternal glory:
Ye have me made whole and sound,
Therefore I will bide by thee in every stound.

Everyman

Welcome, my Good Deeds, now I hear thy voice,
I weep for very sweetness of love.

Knowledge

Be no more sad, but evermore rejoice,
God seeth thy living in His throne above;
Put on this garment to thy behove,
Which with your tears is now all wet,
Lest before God it be unsweet,
When ye to your journey's end come shall.

Everyman

Gentle Knowledge, what do ye it call?

Knowledge

It is the garment of sorrow,
From pain it will you borrow;
Contrition it is,
That getteth forgiveness,
It pleaseth God passing well.

Good Deeds

Everyman, will you wear it for your hele?

Everyman

Now blessed be Jesu, Mary's son;
For now have I on true contrition:
And let us go now without tarrying.
Good Deeds, have we clear our reckoning?

Good Deeds

Yea, indeed, I have here.

Everyman

Then I trust we need not to fear;
Now, friends, let us not depart in twain.

Kindred

Nay, Everyman, that will we not certain.

Good Deeds

Yet must thou lead with thee
Three persons of great might.

Everyman

Who should they be?

Good Deeds

Discretion and Strength they hyght,
And thy Beauty may not abide behind.

Knowledge

Also ye must call to mind
Your Five Wits as for your councillors.

Good Deeds

You must have them ready at all hours.

Everyman

How shall I get them hither?

Kindred

You must call them all together,
And they will hear you incontinent.

Everyman

My friends, come hither, and be present,
Discretion, Strength, my Five Wits and Beauty.

Beauty

Here at your will we be all ready;
What will ye that we should do?

Good Deeds

That ye would with Everyman go,
And help him in his pilgrimage:
Advise you, will ye go with him or not in that voyage?

Strength

We will bring him all thither
To help and comfort him, ye may believe me.

Discretion

So will we go with him altogether.

Everyman

Almighty God, loved may Thou be;
I give Thee laud that I have hither brought
Strength, Discretion, Beauty, Five Wits: lack I
    nought:
And my Good Deeds, with Knowledge clear,

All be in my company at my will here;
I desire no more to my business.

Strength

And I Strength will by you stand in distress,
Though thou wouldest in battle fight on the ground.

Five Wits

And though it were thorow the world round,
We will not depart for sweet ne for sour.

Beauty

No more will I unto death's hour,
Whatsoever thereof befall.

Discretion

Everyman, advise you first of all,
Go with a good advisement and deliberation;
We all give you virtuous monition
That all shall be well.

Everyman

My friends, hark what I will you tell;
I pray God reward you in His heavenly sphere:
Now hearken all that be here;
For I will make my testament
Here before you all present:
In alms half my good I will give with my hands twain
In the way of charity with good intent,
And the other half still shall remain:
I it bequeath to be returned there it ought to be.
This I do in despite of the fiend of hell,
To go quit out of his peril
Ever after this day.

Knowledge

Everyman, hearken what I will say;
Go to priesthood, I you advise,
And receive of him in any wise
The holy sacrament and ointment together,
Then shortly see ye turn again hither,
We will all abide you here.

Five Wits

Yea, Everyman, hie you that ye ready were:
There is no emperor, king, duke, ne baron,
That of God hath commission,
As hath the least priest in the world being;
For of the blessed sacraments pure and benign
He beareth the keys, and thereof hath cure
For man's redemption, it is ever sure,
Which God for our soul's medicine
Gave us out of his heart with great pain,
Here in this transitory life for thee and me:
The blessed sacraments seven there be,
Baptism, confirmation, with priesthood good,
And the sacrament of God's precious flesh and blood,
Marriage, the holy extreme unction, and penance;
These seven be good to have in remembrance,
Gracious sacraments of high divinity.

Everyman

Fain would I receive that holy body,
And meekly to my ghostly father I will go.

Five Wits

Everyman, that is the best that ye can do;
God will you to salvation bring,
For good priesthood exceedeth all other thing;
To us holy scripture they do teach,
And converteth man fro sin heaven to reach;
God hath to them more power given
Than to any angel that is in heaven:
With five words he may consecrate
God's body in flesh and blood to take,
And handleth his Maker between his hands,
The priest bindeth and unbindeth all bands
Both in earth and in heaven;
He ministers all the sacraments seven:
Though we kiss thy feet, thou wert worthy:
Thou art the surgeon that cureth sin deadly,
No remedy may we find under God,
But all only priesthood.
Everyman, God gave priest[s] that dignity,
And setteth them in His stead among us to be;
Thus be they above angels in degree.

Knowledge

If priests be good, it is so surely,
But when Jesu heng on the cross with great smart,
There he gave us out of his blessed heart
The same sacrament in great torment.
He sold them not to us, that Lord omnipotent;
Therefore Saint Peter the Apostle doth say,
That Jesus' curse hath all they,
Which God their Saviour do buy or sell,
Or they for any money do take or tell,
Sinful priests giveth the sinners example bad,
Their children sitteth by other men's fires, I have
      heard,
And some haunteth women's company,
With unclean life, as lusts of lechery;
These be with sin made blind.

Five Wits

I trust to God, no such may we find:
Therefore let us priesthood honour,
And follow their doctrine for our soul's succour;
We be their sheep, and they [our] shepherds be,
By whom we all be kept in surety.
Peace! for yonder I see Everyman come,
Which hath made true satisfaction.

Good Deeds

Methink it is he indeed.

Everyman

Now Jesu Christ be your alder speed!
I have received the sacrament of my redemption,
And then mine extreme unction;
Blessed be all they that counselled me to take it:
And now, friends, let us go without longer respite;
I thank God that ye have tarried so long.
Now set each of you on this rod your hand,
And shortly follow me;
I go before, there I would be:
God be our guide.

Strength

Everyman, we will not fro you go,
Till ye have gone this voyage long.

Discretion

I Discretion will bide by you also.

Knowledge

And though this pilgrimage be never so strong,
I will never part you fro:
Everyman, I will be as sure by thee,
As ever I was by Judas Maccabee.

Everyman

Alas! I am so faint I may not stand,
My limbs under me do fold:
Friends, let us not turn again to this land,
Not for all the world's gold;
For into this cave must I creep.

Beauty

And turn to the earth, and there to sleep.

Everyman

What, into this grave? Alas!

Beauty

Yea, there shall ye consume more and less.

Everyman

And what, should I smother here?
Yea, by my faith, and never more appear;
In this world live no more we shall,
But in heaven before the highest Lord of all.

Beauty

I cross out all this: adieu, by Saint John;
I take my cap in my lap, and am gone.

Everyman

What, Beauty? whither will ye?

Beauty

Peace! I am deaf, I look not behind me,
Not, and thou wouldst give me all the gold in thy
    chest.

Everyman

Alas! whereto may I now trust?
Beauty doth fast away hie:
She promised with me to live and die.

Strength

Everyman, I will thee also forsake and deny,
The game liketh me not at all.

Everyman

Why then ye will forsake me all:
Strength, tarry, I pray you, a little space.

Strength

Nay, sir, by the rood of grace,
I will hie me from thee fast,
Though thou weep till thy heart brast.

Everyman

Ye would ever bide by me, ye said.

Strength

Yea, I have you far enough conveyed:
Ye be old enough, I understand,
Your pilgrimage to take on hand;
I repent me, that I hither came.

Everyman

Strength, you to displease I am to blame;
Yet promise is debt; this ye well wot.

Strength

In faith, as for that I care not:
Thou art but a fool to complain;
Thou spendest thy speech and wasteth thy brain:
Go, thrist thee into the ground.

Everyman

I had ween'd surer I should you have found:
But I see well, he that trusteth in his Strength,
Is greatly deceived at the length;
Both Strength and Beauty hath forsaken me,
Yet they promised me steadfast to be.

Discretion

Everyman, I will after Strength be gone;
As for me, I will leave you alone.

Everyman

Why, Discretion, will ye forsake me?

Discretion

Yea, in faith, I will go fro thee;
For when Strength is gone before,
Then I follow after evermore.

Everyman

Yet, I pray thee, for love of the Trinity,
Look in my grave once piteously.

Discretion

Nay, so nigh will I not come.
Now farewell, fellows everichone.

Everyman

Oh, all thing faileth, save God alone.
Beauty, Strength, and Discretion,
For, when Death bloweth his blast,
They all run fro me full fast.

Five Wits

Everyman, of thee now my leave I take;
I will follow the other, for here I thee forsake.

Everyman

Alas! then may I both wail and weep;
For I took you for my best friend.

Five Wits

I will no lenger thee keep:
Now farewell, and here an end.

Everyman

Now, Jesu, help! all hath forsaken me.

Good Deeds

Nay, Everyman, I will abide with thee,
I will not forsake thee indeed;
Thou shalt find me a good friend at need.

Everyman

Gramercy, Good Deeds, now may I true friends see
They have forsaken me everychone;
I loved them better than my good deeds alone:
Knowledge, will ye forsake me also?

Knowledge

Yea, Everyman, when ye to death shall go;
But not yet for no manner of danger.

Everyman

Gramercy, Knowledge, with all my heart.

Knowledge

Nay, yet I will not from hence depart,
Till I see where ye shall be come.

Everyman

Methinketh, alas! that I must be gone
To make my reckoning, and my debts pay;
For I see my time is nigh spent away.
Take ensample, all ye that this do hear or see,
How they that I loved best now forsake me;
Except my Good Deeds, that bideth truly.

Good Deeds

All earthly things is but vanity,
Beauty, Strength, and Discretion do man forsake,

Foolish friends and kinsmen, that fair spake;
All fleeth save Good Deeds, and that am I.

Everyman

Have mercy on me, God most mighty,
And stand by me, thou mother and maid Mary.

Good Deeds

Fear not, I will speak for thee.

Everyman

Here I cry, God mercy!

Good Deeds

Short our end and minish our pain:
Let us go, and never come again.

Everyman

Into thy hands, Lord, my soul I commend,
Receive it, Lord, that it be not lost;
As thou me boughtest, so me defend,
And save me fro the fiend's boast,
That I may appear with that blessed host
That shall be saved at the day of doom:
In manus tuas, of might most,
For ever commendo spiritum meum.

[*Everyman dies.*]

Knowledge

Now hath he suffered that we all shall endure:
The Good Deeds shall make all sure;
Now hath he made ending.
Methinketh that I hear angels sing,
And make great joy and melody,
Where Everyman's soul shall received be.

The Angel

Come, excellent elect spouse to Jesu,
Here above thou shalt go,
Because of thy singular virtue:
Now thy soul is taken thy body fro,
Thy reckoning is crystal clear;

186

Now shalt thou into the heavenly sphere,
Unto the which all ye shall come
That liveth well, after the day of doom.

Doctor

This memory all men may have in mind;
Ye hearers, take it of worth, old and young,
And forsake pride, for he deceiveth you in the end,
And remember Beauty, Five Wits, Strength, and
    Discretion,
They all at last do Everyman forsake,
Save his Good Deeds; [them he] there doth take:
But beware, for, and they be small,
Before God he hath no help at all;
None excuse may be there for Everyman:
Alas, how shall he do then?
For after death amends may no man make,
For then mercy and pity doth him forsake;
If his reckoning be not clear, when he doth come,
God will say, Ite, maledicti, in ignem æternum;
And he that hath his account whole and sound,
High in heaven he shall be crowned;
Unto which place God bring us all thither,
That we may live body and soul together;
Thereto help the Trinity:
Amen, say ye, for Saint Charity.